Δ Architectural Design

Surface Consciousness

Guest-edited by Mark Taylor

WILEY-ACADEMY

Architectural Design

Vol 73 No 2 Mar/Apr 2003
ISBN 047084843X
Profile No 162

Editorial Offices
International House
Ealing Broadway Centre
London W5 5DB
T: +44 (0)20 8326 3800
F: +44 (0)20 8326 3801
E: architecturaldesign@wiley.co.uk

Editor
Helen Castle
Production
Mariangela Palazzi-Williams
Art Director
Christian Küsters ↪ CHK Design
Designer
Scott Bradley ↪ CHK Design
Picture Editor
Famida Rasheed

Advertisement Sales
01243 843272

Abbreviated positions
b=bottom, c=centre, l=left, r=right

AD
pp 8-19 © Mark Burry; pp 20-25 © Objectile;
pp 26-28 & 29(b) © Horst Kiechle; p 29(t) ©
Misho + Associates; pp 30-35 Mark Taylor; pp
36-7, 40 & 42 © Craig Potton; p 39 © Alexander
Turnbull Library, Wellington, New Zealand; p 43
© Institut für Geschichte und Theorie der
Architektur ETH Zürich; p 44 © Oeffentliche
Kunstsammlung Basel, Martin Bühler; p 45
© Margherita Spiluttini; p 49 © Herzog & de
Meuron; pp 50-56 courtesy Estate of R
Buckminster Fuller; pp 57-8, 59(t) & 60
© Crowd Productions; p 59(c&b) © Crowd
Productions, photos: Michael Trudgeon; p 64(l)
© 2001, The Society of Photo-Optical
Instrumentation Engineers ('Investigating the
Effect of Texture Orientation on the Perception
of 3D Shape' [4299-76], V Interrante and S Kim);
p 64(r) © 1997 IEEE ('Conveying the 3D shape of
smoothly curving transparent surfaces via
texture,' Victoria Interrante, Henry Fuchs and
Stephen Pizer, IEEE, Transactions on
Visualization and Computer Graphics, 3 (2),
April-June 1997, pp 98-117); pp 65-68 courtesy
of the artist and Tolarno Galleries, Melbourne;
pp 69, 71(tx3), 72(cx3), 73(inset & cx3) & 74(b)
© Ashton Raggatt McDougall Pty Ltd; pp 70,
71(c&cr), 72(t) & 73(t) © Ashton Raggatt
McDougall Pty Ltd, photos: John Gollings;
p 72(inset) © Ashton Raggatt McDougall Pty Ltd,
photo: Peter Bennetts; p 74(t&c) © Ashton
Raggatt McDougall Pty Ltd, photo: Brent
Allpress; pp 75-6, 77(t), 78-9 © Lyons, photos:
John Gollings; p 80(l) © Lyons; p 80(tr) © Lyons,
photo: Trevor Mein; p 80(br) courtesy of the
Museum of Contemporary Art, Sydney; pp 81-5
© Julieanna Preston; pp 86-7 photos: © John
Gollings; pp 88-9 © Minifie Nixon.

AD+
pp 94-5+ & 96+(tl) © Paul Warchol /
photography by Paul Warchol; p 96+(c&b)
© Craig Kellogg; pp 97+ & 99+(tr&b) courtesy
Ushida Findlay, photos: James Harris; pp 98+,
99+(t) & 102+ courtesy Ushida Findlay; pp 100-
101+ courtesy Ushida Findlay, photos:
Katshuhisa Kida; pp 103+, 105+, 108+(b) & 109+
© Lab + Bates Smart; pp 106+(t) & 108+(tl)
photos: © Trevor Mein; p 108+(cr) photo:
© Peter Clarke; pp 110-118+ © Mark Burry;
p120+(tl) © 2001 Dorothy Alexander; p 120+(bl)
© Caples Jefferson; p 120+(br) courtesy Caples
Jefferson, © Albert Vecerka Photography;
p 121+(l) Ezra Stoller © Esto; pp 122+(r), 123-5+
© Cecil Balmond, illustrations from informal -
designed with Jannuzzi Smith, published by
Prestel; pp 126-7+ © The Building Exploratory.

Cover image by Mark Burry

**James Carpenter Design Associates
+ Toshiko Mori Architect**

In the Practice Profile, 'James Carpenter
Design Associates + Toshiko Mori Architect'
(Jan/Feb 2003) a number of factual or
technical errors appeared in the article and
we wish to correct these as follows:

- the image of the Lens Ceiling for the
Federal Building and Courthouse, Phoenix,
was duplicated on the left-hand side of the
page, where the image of the Glass Walls
and Roof for the Columbus Centre should
have appeared;
- the credit for Tulane University Student
Center should have read in full as Vincent
James Associates Architects with James
Carpenter Design Associates, Inc;
- the roof of the Tulane University Student
Center is made of metal rather than glass;
- Toshiko Mori collaborated on the Issey
Miyake shop, Pleats Please, in New York's
SoHo, with Nicolas Gwaenel, not James
Carpenter;
- Toshiko Mori's thesis at the Cooper Union
was for a 165 square foot rather than a 1000
square foot prototype retail display;
- The boutique at Bendel's was for Comme
des Garcons, not Issey Miyake, and it did not
incorporate fibreglass;
- In 1987, Toshiko Mori collaborated with
Shiro Kuramata on an Issey Miyake store at
77th Street and Madison Avenue, New York,
which was later replaced in 1996 by the shop
described in the article;
- Toshiko Mori used block, not brick, in the
Cohen Guesthouse, but not the Ocala block
that Paul Rudolph used in the main house;
- the Coast Guard dormitory on the grounds
of the Silverstein House was converted to a
guesthouse, not a pool house, and is located
88 feet from the main house;
- the exterior photograph of the Leaming
House was of the house previous to
renovations;
- the garage of the Leaming House is made
out of galvanised steel; the stainless steel
columns and clerestory are in the main
house;
-on the sloped (not curved) roof of the Talbot
house, snow is melted solely by heat
collected on the black roof surface, not by
hot air within the house;
- Toshiko Mori did not raise the $100,000 for
the student competition for a fence around
the construction site for Pei Cobb Freed's
social science building at Harvard, an
existing University budget was drawn upon.

Subscription Offices UK
John Wiley & Sons Ltd.
Journals Administration Department
1 Oldlands Way, Bognor Regis
West Sussex, PO22 9SA
T: +44 (0)1243 843272
F: +44 (0)1243 843232
E: cs-journals@wiley.co.uk

Annual Subscription Rates 2003
Institutional Rate: UK £160
Personal Rate: UK £99
Student Rate: UK £70
Institutional Rate: US $240
Personal Rate: US $150
Student Rate: US $105
AD is published bi-monthly.
Prices are for six issues and include
postage and handling charges.
Periodicals postage paid at Jamaica,
NY 11431. Air freight and mailing
in the USA by Publications
Expediting Services Inc, 200 Meacham
Avenue, Elmont, NY 11003

Single Issues UK: £22.50
Single Issues outside UK: US $45.00
Details of postage and packing charges
available on request

Postmaster
Send address changes to AD Publications
Expediting Services, 200 Meacham Avenue,
Elmont, NY 11003

Printed in Italy. All prices are subject
to change without notice.
[ISSN: 0003-8504]

8
20
26
36
43
50
57
69

103+
110+
122+

126+

4   Editorial   *Helen Castle*

5   Introduction   *Mark Taylor*

8   Between Surface and Substance   *Mark Burry*

20   Philibert de L'Orme Pavilion: Towards an Associative Architecture   *Bernard Cache*

26   Amorphous Structures   *Horst Kiechle*

30   Surface-Talk   *Mark Taylor*

36   Volcanic Matter: The Architecture of Whakaari/White Island   *Sarah Treadwell*

43   Masked Matter and Other Diagrams   *Hans Frei*

50   From Microcosm to Macrocosm: The Surface of Fuller and Sadao's US Pavilion at Montreal Expo '67   *Timothy M. Rohan*

57   In Search of the Plasma Membrane   *Michael Trudgeon*

61   Conveying 3-D Shape and Depth with Textured and Transparent Surfaces   *Victoria Interrante*

65   Sticks and Stones: Skins and Bones   *Peter Wood*

69   Ornamental Operations   *Brent Allpress*

75   Seduction, Subversion and Predation: Surface Characteristics   *Michael J Ostwald*

81   Sewing Surface: Ground Matters Beneath the Eiffel Tower   *Julieanna Preston*

86   Surface: Architecture's Expanded Field   *Karen Burns*

92   Contributor Biographies

Surface Consciousness
Guest-edited by Mark Taylor

94+   Interior Eye **Deluxe Apartments in the Sky** *Craig Kellogg*

97+   Practice Profile **Kathryn Findlay of Ushida Findlay** *Neil Spiller*

103+   Building Profile **Federation Square, Melbourne** *Jeremy Melvin*

110+   Engineering Exegesis **Blurring the Lines: Mediating between analogue and digital skill sets** *Mark Burry*

119+   Highlights from Wiley Academy *Jane Peyton*

120+   Congratulations to Jayne Merkel *Helen Castle*

122+   Invisibly Informal *Lucy Bullivant*

126+   Site Lines **Building Exploratory** *Hannah Ford*

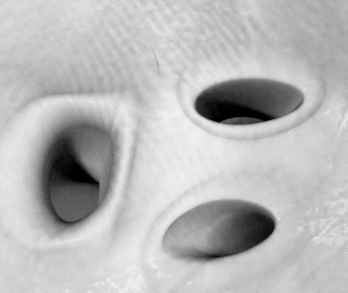

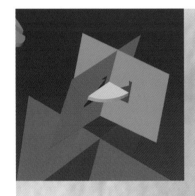

For the last few years, it has been part of *Architectural Design*'s remit to push forward the debate surrounding experimental digital architecture. This has primarily focused on the challenge to realise built works with the aid of digital tools, focusing on contemporary techniques (no 1, vol 72, 2002) or the potential of prototyping through Versioning (no 5, vol 72, 2002); this is shored up by this year's engineering series in △ Plus, 'Blurring the Lines' (see p 110), which explicitly explores the issues surrounding computer-aided manufacture. 'Surface Consciousness', however, represents a deeper dig into the philological shifts that are occurring with the onset of digital techniques and representations. The polarisation of ornament and structure that were first cast in stone by Vitruvius and perpetuated by the modernists no longer holds up. Computer modelling of integrated surfaces has usurped this bifurcation by blurring the inside and outside, requiring new ways of considering tectonic form. In this issue the challenge is spearheaded by Mark Taylor's own article, 'Surface-Talk', in which he explores the ideas of the philosopher Avrum Stroll, who has introduced new ways of perceiving surface more relevant to mathematical and architectural developments. The purpose of this issue is not, however, solely cerebral. It is also a celebration of the full range of surface forms and effects. Freed from the most onerous of modernist spectres, the extraneous or the decorative, architects such as Herzog & de Meuron, Michael Trudgeon, Ashton Raggatt McDougall (ARM) and Lyons are proving themselves able to pursue the sensuous, diagrammatic and even the ornamental with a vengeance. △

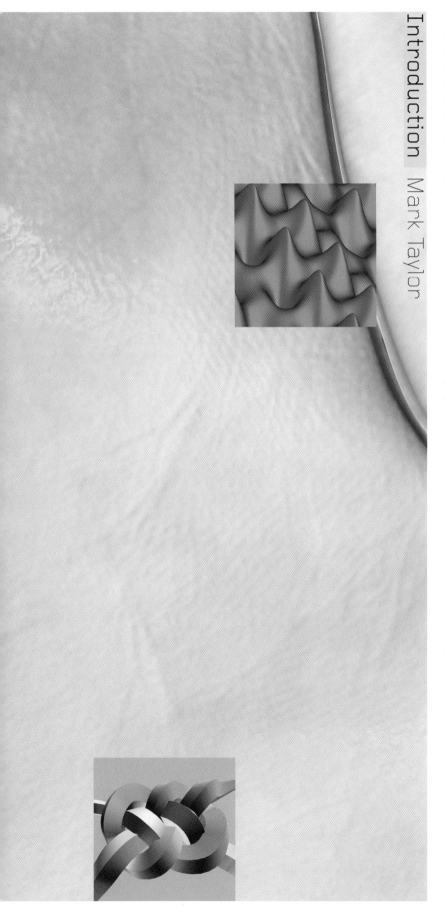

Introduction Mark Taylor

The work presented in this issue of *Architectural Design* focuses on surface in an effort to recognise a spatial condition that lies outside the traditional architectural models that polarise surface and substrate. Shifting between digital constructions of surface, computer science imaging, built realisation and theoretical aspects of surface, issues of surface transparency, articulation and stability are brought to the fore. The focus is on surface as the subject of study rather than the oppositional formation of whether surface is depth or depth is surface, or the phrenologist's ability to strip away surface to find hidden depths.

For some contributors surface is investigated as a meaningful relationship between contemporary methods of visioning, making and fabricating. Other papers discuss contemporary perceptions of surface relative to historical and theoretical frameworks, and the slippage that occurs between 'surface' and 'skin'. To assist this I have included a discussion of one aspect of Avrum Stroll's book *Surfaces* – his conceptions of surface as abstraction and physical entity. Probing surface relative to depth, Stroll shifts from surface-as-interface to surface-as-molecular; a position also found in the writings of Semper and Alberti, enabling their work to be recast within the same framework.

In recent years many digitally based projects have rejected linear perspective, a tyranny that Henri Lefevbre argues fetishised the facade: 'a volume made up of planes and lent spurious depth by means of decorative motives'.[1] Removing the observer from a fixed point in space, these digital works destabilise the stable visual world born out of gravity, proportion and Euclidian rationality. They cannot be understood as an oppositional dualism between surface and structure for many are conceived as surface, as structure. Their various algorithmic methods of finding form necessarily alter how we view the architecture. If once buildings were conceived additively, as a collection of surfaces, projections and motifs, there is now a desire to conceive them as surface.

To this extent the relationship between surface and substance in design and manufacturing is addressed by both Mark Burry and Bernard Cache. Where Burry seeks equivalence in design creativity through the real and tangible (rather than the escape into cyberspace), Cache discusses how the abstract surfaces of the projective cube of his Philibert de L'Orme Pavilion can be brought into 'automatised' design through CAD software. In effect both architects are concerned with the digital information lying behind the design, and how the design can be varied throughout the process. Freeing themselves from what Deleuze and Guattari call 'arborescent' models of architecture – 'tree-pillars, branch-beams, foliage vaults'[2] – they engage with architectural surface as mathematics, questioning

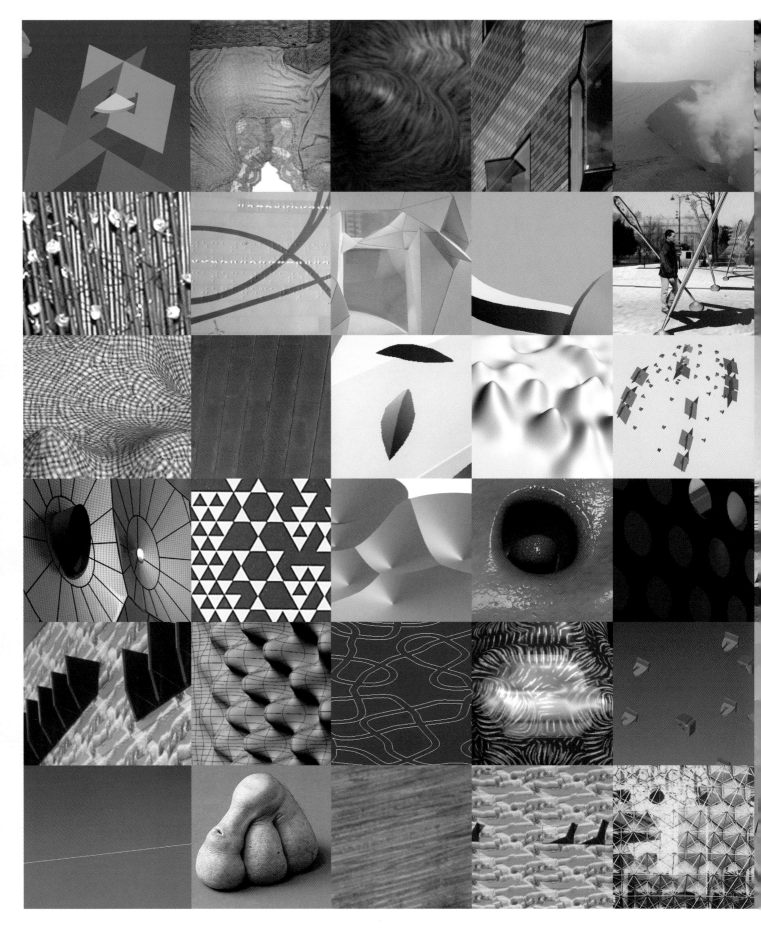

the relationship between pure geometry and built approximations, between inside and outside, one side and the other. Cache discusses this through his interest in interlacings of the rood screen and knot theory (topology), whereas Burry's interest lies in the resolution of surface instability brought about by unstable topographies of the paramorph, the hyposurface and the 'perplication'.

Horst Kiechle's work focuses on the creation of amorphous constructions comprised of nonregular surfaces. In this work subtle shifts in each surface challenge the regularising of space through crystalline geometry. Notions of surface and spatial instability continue in the essay by Sarah Treadwell where the difficult occupation of a volcanic terrain occurs along a shifting boundary between matter and nonexistence. Caught on the crater's edge between substance and vapour, foundational strategies of stable ground and nurturing dark interiority dissipate in flames. This hissing, heaving, horizontal surface poses similar theoretical challenges to boundaries of physical space, as does dECOi's Aegis Hyposurface in the vertical plane. These two primary moves – the horizontal and the vertical – are discussed by Hans Frei as a virtual movement of matter rather than a technical manipulation of surface movement. His discussion of Herzog & de Meuron's Eberswalde library (contextualised by a Semperian sense of the cosmetic) reveals an architectural surface that is nonrepresentational – a diagrammatic surface.

Four essays examine thin-skin transparent or translucent surfaces. Of these, three concern contemporary attitudes to surface created by thin-skin digital representation, whereas the fourth, by Tim Rohan, traces Buckminster Fuller's fluid geography of the Dymaxion Map into the 1967 Montreal Expo dome. Predating transparent digital models this three-quarters transparent sphere was sealed by thousands of acrylic plastic minidomes. Though Fuller's skin was likened to the skin of an orange or animal skin, he was interested in how a surface could mimic the sensitivity of the human skin – letting in light, porosity etc, and could operate as an animated smart surface.

Increasingly we have seen 'smart surface' become digital screen, particularly where large sections of a building's envelope are substituted for digital transmitters. But for Michael Trudgeon, smart surface is not the smart

programmable 'transmitters' suggested by Alicia Imperiale,[3] but is a place of information exchange. Trudgeon's thin-skin plasma membrane is an attempt to build the thin translucent surface favoured by digital rendering, and is realised as a discontinuous and fragmented porous surface of several layers. It is not the 'literal transparency' that uses glass, but is what Colin Rowe refers to as 'phenomenal transparency' – transparency turned into opacity.[4]

While it is necessary to avoid the former since it is solution-based not problem-based, the very real problem of the dissolution of figure-ground relationships and the inevitable spatial oscillations that occur with digital transparency are confronted in the work of Victoria Interrante. Her work recognises the difficulty of our ability to perceive smoothly finished transparent surfaces as a very real problem of spatial understanding. This surface is, as Peter Wood acknowledges in his essay, a primary architectural state that can be understood as an artificial membrane rather than a dermis. Cast from the body as a postcoital condom, the digital skin is regarded as wholly ornamental for it displaces the traditional architectural skin for a 'textured' artificial construction.

Ashton Raggatt McDougall (ARM) take hold of this position on ornament and return it with a vengeance through misappropriation and recurring cultural concerns. Brent Allpress reviews ARM's use of ornament as operative abstraction in which cultural conventions of ornament give way to the cutting, marking and layering of shaped surfaces. Visual textures offer a surface tactility that creates an optical illusion demanding touch – a moment Michael Ostwald also observes in the work of Lyons where the form of the building and the impression generated by its skin are at variance. There is a transfiguration of surface materiality.

Julieanna Preston suggests that ground (earth) resists being reduced to an abstraction; it is neither a line, a coating, nor an in-between spacer. Her project to fashion a new landscape surface beneath the Eiffel Tower therefore probes the depth of surface. It utilises techniques and practices of sewing to manipulate surface as material having spatial depth – ground as a deep surface.

Karen Burns takes a self-reflexive journey around surface, reminding us that to rethink the role and power of surface necessitates invoking its others, those things that structure the definition of surface. This is a timely reminder of what Julia Kristeva calls a crisis in relation to contemporary art-forms and the necessary reconnection of the visible with the invisible.[5] ⚙

Notes
1. Henri Lefebvre, *The Production of Space*, trans Donald Nicholson-Smith, Blackwell (Oxford), 1992, p 361.
2. Gilles Deleuze and Félix Guattari, *A Thousand Plateaus: Capitalism and Schizophrenia*, University of Minnesota Press (Minneapolis and London), 1987, p 329.
3. Alicia Imperiale, *New Flatness, Surface Tension in Digital Architecture*, Birkhäuser (Basel, Boston and Berlin), 2000, p 22.
4. Colin Rowe and Robert Slutsky, 'Transparency: literal and phenomenal', *The Mathematics of the Ideal Villa and Other Essays*, MIT Press (Cambridge, Mass), 1996.
5. Julia Kristeva, 'Institutional interdisciplinarity in theory and practice: an interview', in Alex Coles and Alexia Defert (eds) *The Anxiety of Interdisciplinarity*, Backless Books (London), 1998.

Between Surface and Substance

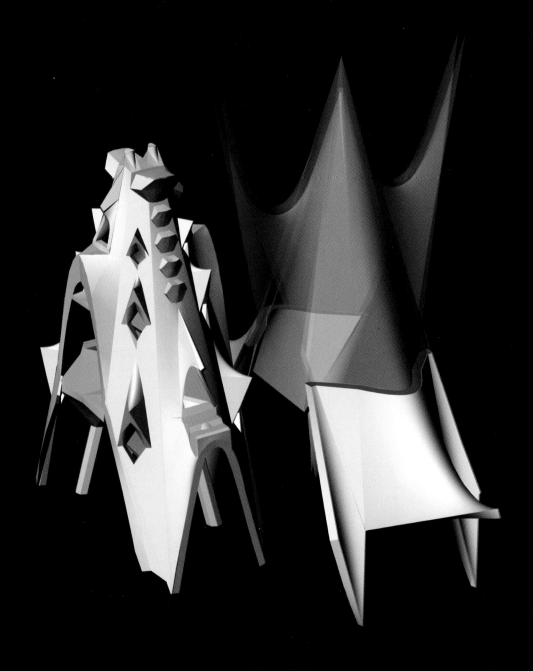

What lies between form as style and architectural realisation in material form? Can digitally conceived buildings exhibit the same 'truth to materials' – 'a brick be a brick' – as their modernist predecessors? Mark Burry takes us on an exploration of the territory that lies between surface and substance. At a time when the conceptual dominates in art and architecture and the intellect resides over physical craft, he strives for a new resolution between the virtual and the material. Describing four projects – two Euclidean and two non-Euclidean – Burry proposes that the most fertile arena for re-engagement lies in mathematics.

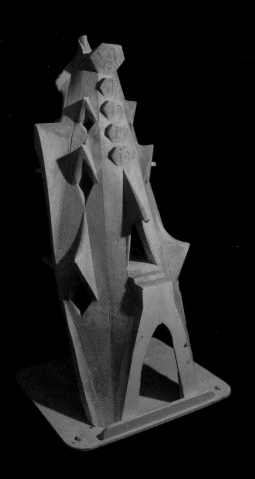

Sagrada Família Church, Antoni Gaudí, building commenced 1882 – Mark Burry (Consultant Architect) with Jordi Bonet (Coordinating Architect and Director) and Jordi Faulí (Project Architect).

Opposite
Digital version of the model shown in the image on the right placed next to a part cut away geometrical interpretation showing the hyperbolic paraboloid external surfaces. If the outside surfaces are composed (in the main) from hyperbolic paraboloids, then the interior surface is not when uniform wall thickness is assumed. In terms of the facility of construction, the exterior ruled surfaces (hyperbolic paraboloids) have been privileged, yet in practical terms, through gravity, the interior surface moulds (which are not ruled surfaces) will dominate the construction process.

Above
Part of the Sagrada Família Church nave roof by Gaudí, modelled at a scale of 1:25 in gypsum plaster.

I am interested in understanding more about the territory lying between treating form as merely a *superficial* condition and its tectonic substantiation. Within this territory I wish to locate insights into the technical and philosophical implications that enhanced virtual treatments bring to the visual representation of the real. These insights have been gained through four projects at the forefront of developing digital craft. By 'superficial' I refer to the qualities of appearance that can be read as being part of a set often referred to as 'style': Neoclassical or Gothic, for instance. 'Tectonically substantiated' refers to modernist orthodoxies including Khan's bricks speaking of being bricks, built fabric exhibiting 'truth to materials', and other related principles that insist on the surface of any construction being the conscious expression of the actual materials and fabrication techniques employed. This orthodoxy is compromised by digitally created visual representations of substance where an expression of material truth is potentially meaningless: I am comparing a digital model with a physical model here.

The conceptualisation of any architectural form and space is not necessarily contingent on initial or subsequent digital intervention as a route to physical production. Modernist orthodoxy, however, cannot simply be rejected as an inadequate philosophy for our time. As virtual representation of what we feel to be real further intrudes into our culture and the concomitant education of architects, the need to understand more about the land between surface and substance becomes somewhat acute.

A Search for New Formal Engagement
There is a temptation to regard tectonics, materiality and free form as uniquely contemporary questions related to new formal challenges. New tools allegedly give us the possibility of producing the Guggenheim in Bilbao as if Gaudí had not suspended a network of weights to give form to the Colònia Güell Church (1898–1916), Rudolf Steiner had not laboured successfully on the description and construction of the preposterous second iteration of his Goetheanum (1924–28),[1] Le Corbusier on the chapel at Ronchamp, France (1956), Eero Saarinen on the TWA Building (1962), Hans Sharoun on the Berlin Philharmonic (1963), all during the last century. In looking at how best to assimilate new tools such as the animation algorithms included within popular rendering packages (note how disingenuous the software manufacturers are in describing digital representation tools in the equivalent terms as 'stucco'), we can benefit from delving back into earlier quests for appropriate form for our age.

My principal source is Eliel Saarinen's *The Search for Form: A Fundamental Approach to Art,* first

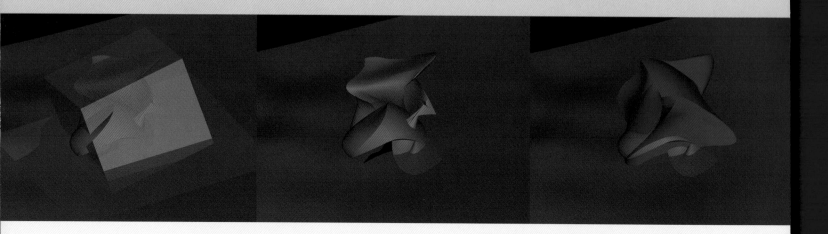

published in 1948.[2] Saarinen sees that educating architects to conform to any particular style reduces the art of composition to rule-based decision making and, at worst, downgrades architects to informed copyists. Written in three parts, *The Search for Form* provides an overview and analysis firstly of the history of Western architecture and the influence of mechanisation, secondly of creativity, organic principles, dynamism and the relationship between form and time, and concludes with a consideration of reason and sensation. In this work, Saarinen ponders the role of conceptual art:

> Yet in some circles there seems to be a strange inclination to produce art by virtue of some sort of esoteric knowledge. Many see fit to recognize art – to be sure, art of the most 'sublime order' – as something deeply mysterious, something enigmatically transcendental, understandable only by the selected few. Such an attitude of exaggerated self-consciousness – where the artist himself [sic] frequently plays the role of an innocent tool in the hands of purveyors of esthetic intricacy and commercial humbug – brings art easily into artificial depths and self-deceptive snobbishness.[3]

At the time of writing, the Institute of Contemporary Arts – a major cultural and educational institution in the UK – has dealt swiftly with Ivan Massow's denouncement of 'conceptual art' and has sacked him as the institute's director. Writing about aspects of his dismissal, Massow responded with:

> Although they 'get' conceptual art, and are passionate about art, my words have struck a resonant chord in articulating something they've never dared say before. They want

substance, they want elevation, they want ... 'craft'. Yes, craft ... just when it seemed that the establishment was no longer shockable, out it jumped – to send them all into a frenzy ... Is it time for the philosophical underpinnings of conceptual art to be challenged? It is built on a nihilistic philosophical foundation. Kant's theory of the 'sublime' elevates the 'formless' and 'shocking'. Personally, I'm about ready now for some form and substance.[4]

Also in the UK, some months later, the substantial Paul Hamlyn Foundation prize was awarded for a work by Ceal Floyer titled 'Rubbish Bag', filled, one presumes, with rubbish – an iconic presumption, because it was apparently filled with nothing other than air:

> Floyer's work in Sunderland is a black bin-liner full of air, slumped on the floor. It reminds us that context and placement is everything, and that the slightest, most abject gesture can be resonant. Floyer's bag of air makes me think of bodies, death, futility, emptiness, waste. Its starkness is overwhelming.[5]

One gathers that it was this particular issue, the nature of its contents being obscured by the deliberate opacity of the enclosing membrane (for rubbish is meant to be invisible) that intellectually engaged the viewers: there is the *frisson* of being forced to confront the implications of any presumption that the rubbish bag must contain rubbish, whereas it might not indeed contain rubbish at all ... Such caustic irony can be claimed as a metaphor for social stereotyping, for instance, or the way we judge books by their covers, woods by their trees and, not least, architectural substance through its surfaces. With this and similar 'conceptual' work we are encouraged to separate skill, artistry, craft and material value from other valid intellectual perspectives. 'Rubbish Bag' is a quite different container, say, than a Fabergé egg (when it is

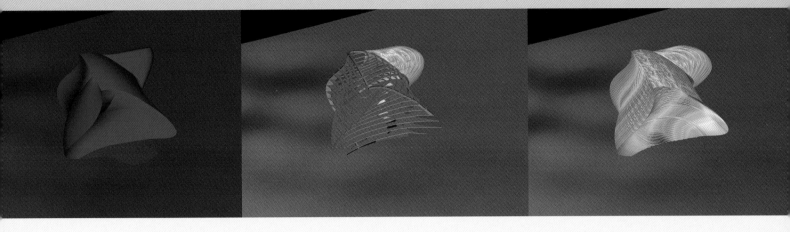

closed, what surprise does it hold?) which beyond its skilful artifice may not equate to the same level of intellectual commitment nor equal the bravado of publicly exhibiting a utilitarian rubbish sack *manqué* crafted only so far as to reveal aspects of ourselves that otherwise go unchallenged.

This question of the value of art versus cost has, of course, been with us since the Industrial Revolution, and becomes predominant with cyclical regularity. Following is what Saarinen had to say about superficiality with regard to valuing form (as artistic endeavour) in 1948:

> Now then, what is form? Which are its primary characteristics? Is form an intelligible product of outer shape, apparent to the outer eye only? Or is there a deeper meaning infused into form from sources beyond man's [sic] apprehension? Or, to put it thus: is art soulless; or does it have a soul. The answer is obvious. However, because there exists an abundance of forms that are destitute of meaning and yet are regarded as forms of art nay, in many circles as forms of art of the highest excellence – we might just as well at the very outset eliminate from our analysis those cases where form has its origin – soullessly and superficially – from other sources than those that can produce truly genuine art.[6]

Against a backdrop, then, of privileging idea over art in contemporary cultural production, that is, mind over matter, the following four projects consider aspects in the search for form that have a common thread: an engagement with mathematics at some level. In both the digital and traditional domains they represent aspects of mind over matter in a different way.

'Reading Room', Student project set in combined course managed by MIT (Larry Sass) and RMIT University (Mark Burry) with input from Gehry Partners LLP (Jim Glymph and Dennis Shelden). Initial design Dominique Ng (RMIT) taken to detailed resolution by Julian Canterbury (RMIT), Alison Fairley (RMIT), Joy Hou (MIT), Xiaoyi Ma (MIT), Kyle Steinfeld (MIT) 2002.

Above
From the original Phileban geometry to reading room: interior and exterior paramorphs adapted from the cube and cylinder archetypes. The surfaces in the original proposal self-intersect: the original surface (red) interpenetrates through Cartesian accident but was subsequently corrected for the purposes of construction through parametric manipulation, 'tweaked' to rid all self- and interior–exterior surface intersections.

Euclidean 1: Gaudí and the Nave Roof for the Sagrada Família Church

Fragments survive of a 1:25 scaled model of the nave roof for the Sagrada Família Church that coyly disguise their mathematical cladding. Published in 1928, two years after his colleague's death, Rafols wrote the following in what was the first biography of Gaudí:

> Los paraboloids también forman las cubiertes de la nave central y unen los puntos culminantes (70 metros) con los frontones con que terminan los ventinales de la nave central.
> (The hyperbolic paraboloids also form the roof to the central nave and the coincidents points (70 metres) join the gambles over the central nave clerestory windows).[7]

The geometry referred to in the quote and captured by the model is a second-order Euclidean construct that assists description towards construction: ruled surfaces. What is of interest here is its sublimation and masking through artful embellishment of the surfaces with perturbations and openings, and the disappearance of the key piece of information alluded to in Rafols' text: that the surfaces (mainly) are comprised of contiguous hyperbolic paraboloids, all of which have vertices at a common virtual point in space above the centre of the bay. We can show that the digital remodelling of the roof, and the parametrically derived iterations that seek solutions to this situation, have all the component surfaces that conform to Gaudí's codex.

The issue of why Gaudí chose to move exclusively into a world of hyperbolic geometry is covered elsewhere.[8] In this case we can emphasise the virtual point to which the assembled hyperbolic paraboloids converge, its virtuality and its role in the schema, not least providing the necessary clues to latter-day collaborators based far from the building site.

The constituent hyperbolic paraboloids are ruled surfaces – rulings between two non-coplanar lines form the surfaces. This makes for surprisingly easy

description for construction. Indeed, the lower third of the roof was built from spatial information showing coordinates, with the various straight lines linking them shown in colour codes, all presented on a single A3 sheet. To build, the makers simply locate sufficient straight lines that are the edges of adjoining surfaces, divide them equally with an appropriate number of points, join the points virtually in space and render real through the addition of material. In this case the artefact is a full-size plaster maquette produced in the same way that the model-makers produced models for Gaudí. The maquette became the master to make glass-fibre moulds for the in situ roof structure.

The surface of the roof is the interface between that region of the building and the sky. As geometry, and in the context of materiality even at the scale of the ultimate atomic skin, the best we can say is that the surface has impossible material thinness – impossible because the atoms have thickness and are shown elsewhere in this journal to form a rough not smooth surface. In other words, beyond mathematics the surface cannot be pure geometry, only an approximation, albeit well within the tolerances of human visual acuity. Even if we accept this approximation, a problem lies deeper within: what about the interior roof surface?

For this example, structural considerations of the roof determine a uniform thickness. Using the computer we can offset each constituent hyperbolic paraboloid by a given amount, and extend and trim as required to produce a surface of equal litheness as its companion exterior, though without the beneficial rulings of a ruled surface: an offset ruled surface is not of itself a ruled surface. A ruled surface for both the exterior and interior cannot produce an even thickness of separation in any circumstances

unless the surface happened to be flat. So, on the exterior we have the relatively easily executed ruled surface, whereas on the interior we do not. Typically, some would argue, the exterior has been privileged over the interior – odd when we consider the position of the moulds with respect to gravity.

Beyond these physical and pragmatic considerations lie philosophical considerations. If we base any architectural surface on Euclidean geometry, then its companion surface, be it interior or exterior, will not conform to an equivalent geometry without some compromises. The only exception to this is the surface to some homogeneous mass of substance the interior surface of which does not exist or has the thickness of medieval castle walls, for instance. Take as an example a wall treated as a minimal surface or skin. Skin has thickness: if the minimal surface geometry is the centre line of any section through the skin, the physical surfaces themselves will not be minimal. Pure geometry is, of itself, becoming a misrepresentation of the facts, thus when forming any architectural surface it will probably be compromised by the stuff of building.

Euclidean 2: Paramorphs

A recent studio project involving staff and students from Gehry Partners, MIT and the Royal Melbourne Institute of Technology (RMIT) considered the implications of introducing parametric design into the design studio as a collaborative tool.[9] In an effort to constrain the parametric adventure to realistic proportions, given the complexities of introducing students to entirely new ways of working, the project (a reading room situated in the Melbourne Botanical Gardens) was kept relatively simple in terms of programme, but nevertheless sophisticated in all other respects (the nature of reading, public/private arguments, the interior in a public setting etc).

Students were encouraged to work with three parametrically configured paramorphs: two Phileban forms (a cylinder and cube) and a terrain. Paramorphs are forms that have consistent topology but unstable

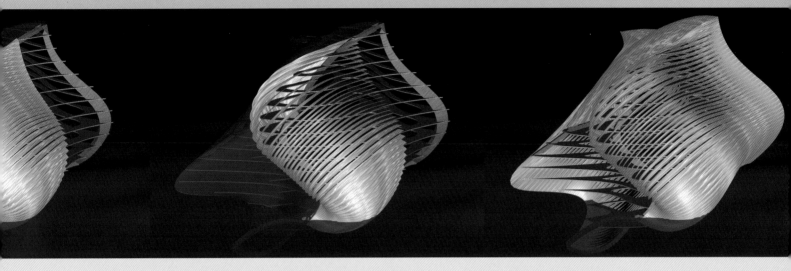

topography: a teacup and a toroid are classic examples – objects with different forms but which can be given equivalent properties. The first two Phileban solids were to be the basis of an interior and exterior surface to the reading room, while the terrain was to be adapted to suit the site and the location of the reading room.

The design of Dominique Ng (RMIT) was taken to detailed resolution by Julian Canterbury (RMIT), Alison Fairley (RMIT), Kyle Steinfeld (MIT), Xiaoyi Ma (MIT) and Joy Hou (MIT). The project was in two parts. The first part involved individual responses to the brief followed by teams of five from both the participating universities formed to take selected projects through to detailed resolution as 'digital mock-ups'. In the second part, the original design authors were not part of the teams taking projects from schematic to detailed resolution. The removal of the conceptual designer from the production team allowed the re-evaluation of the design authorship roles of team members and the digital contribution to complex design processes such as this. Can team members share parameters for a design in common ownership?

From the beginning the project revealed interesting cyber-real implications, especially the propensity for the interior paramorph to both self-intersect and intersect inconveniently with the exterior paramorph. Intriguing as virtual conditions, self-intersections proved to be impossible to resolve as physical mock-ups. The self-intersection is bounded by a line of impossible thinness, and this situation could not be resolved by plaiting or weaving the constituent materials. The parametric nature of the design meant that the morphing of the original forms could be tweaked such that surfaces were not self-intersecting, and by iterative operations a result was assured that remained true to the

original designer's intentions but nevertheless conformed to physical constraints. This correction in itself seemed to sponsor new critical sensibilities about the fragile nature of surfaces once they become mathematically driven entities conforming to Cartesian constructs. Final proposals were shown as a combination of rendered images and physical scale models.

All the surfaces were highly permeable, louvred arrangements inspired apparently by Herzog & de Meuron's treatment of their railway signal box at Auf dem Wolf in Basel (1989–94). The intention of this approach was to mediate between the inside and outside, both environmentally as well as philosophically. The derivation of the louvres was through the division of the parametrically warped sides of the original paramorph by a requisite number of isoparms,[10] a function therefore of the mathematical definition of the surface. The almost organic nature of the openings between adjacent louvres was emphasised by their adjustability in accordance with the positions of key points along each length, relative to their position along the length of the louvre and order in the overall height of the wall. For instance, in a matter of a few seconds the entire character of a louvred face could change from equal openings along the whole length to uniform swelling along the lengths towards the middle, to accentuating the openings at the geographical centre of each face tapering away to being closed at the top, bottom and side boundaries.

The first level of surface instability resulted from the Euclidean geometry of the parent paramorphs corrupted through numerical operations within the parametric design. The second level is the lacerating of the external surface, which melds with the internal through the ambivalence of the louvred construction. The only telling relationship between the exterior and interior surfaces is derived from the separating substance. The secondary structure supporting and separating the louvred faces to the building is a series of horizontal plates, evenly spaced and spanning

'Reading Room', Student project set in combined course managed by MIT (Larry Sass) and RMIT University (Mark Burry) with input from Gehry Partners LLP (Jim Glymph and Dennis Shelden). Initial design Dominique Ng (RMIT) taken to detailed resolution by Julian Canterbury (RMIT), Alison Fairley (RMIT), Joy Hou (MIT), Xiaoyi Ma (MIT), Kyle Steinfeld (MIT) 2002.

Above
Examples of alternative louvre settings for one of the reading room faces, cut away to show the effect.

between the vertical-edge columns that form the main structure to the reading room. The derivation of the horizontal structure is therefore slices through the invisible substance of the walls existentialised and rendered visible.

Non-Euclidean 1: Perplications

Perplication: *Différence et repetition*.
Deleuze offers the term 'perplication' to describe not so much an interweaving as 'cross-foldings' between complex repetitions.[11] The word is coined from the conjunction of 'perplex' and 'plication'. It is the visualisation of concurrent ideas that appear to be the same yet different at the same time. As ideas mature in time, they can be represented as instantiations – blips on the radar screen. They are developments of a theme, self-intersecting prominences and subversions occurring at different times in any muse while maintaining a common thread. In other words, the visual representation is a pictorialisation of our mental space.

Rather than regard our thoughts and theories as part of a linear continuum, we might regard them as forming a landscape of turmoil where subconscious and conscious ideals and desires interweave. In rendering this landscape as a perplication, I am positing this as a continuum having no lateral boundaries, in which subconscious thoughts interweave through each other, emerging as the conscious anywhere that it becomes uncovered. This rendering is therefore an extracted section from this landscape, a liminal representation of a state of mind not necessarily calm at any particular time.

Our cognitive capacity almost insists on physical substantiation of the construct: in rendering the perplication, one is drawn to the (near) impossibility of creating a physical artefact despite the visual representation as a digital rendering appearing to be so tangible. This lie – a continuum, not a surface, and not actually a material possibility – is provoked further by the pretence that the perplications are possible by realistic digital rendering. Using the same surface algorithms, alternative apparent materialisations can be 'realised' as diaphanous cross-folded unravelled bolts of silk or, in contrast, as an impossible alloy of metals that conform to a non-Euclidean regime but obstinately remain immiscible, as some metals in fact are. As images, these perplications are no more than captured moments frozen in time, examples of digital interventions within the tectonic, mathematical derivations from the imagination and not any real physical experience.

Non-Euclidean 2: Hyposurface

In a competition held in early 1999, the Birmingham Hippodrome in the UK invited entries for an 'art/architecture' embellishment for a prominent wall that sailed away from the proposed new foyer 5 metres above the pavement over the heads of passing pedestrians. The wall measures approximately 8 metres across by 7 high. Rather than offer an intervention as some kind of appliqué, dECOi Architects (Mark Goulthorpe) proposed that the wall itself should be the intervention. In line with dECOi's commitment to loose-fit project-based teams, their response to the competition was the assembly of a project team that was a mix of architects, mathematicians, computer programmers and multimedia experts.[12] The team was dispersed over four countries, 18,000 kilometres apart, and neither at the time nor subsequently have all the team members ever met in the same physical space. I believe that this proposal, and the subsequent reconciliation between ideas of augmenting our sensorial environment and the physical control of the surfaces that shape the world, represents one of the few instances of an art piece that can exist only because of digital technology. That is to say, without digital technology, the Aegis Hyposurface could not have been created.

This idea innovated in at least two significant ways. Firstly, it democratised the art piece inasmuch as the hyposurface 'wall', in itself, is neutrally and passively flat until made to inflect in/on itself through the injection of information via what dECOi has described as an electronic central nervous system: stimuli are picked up by sensors responsive to video, sound, light, heat, movement, (whatever), and used to activate the wall surface. Secondly, being probably the world's first interactive physical surface, it calls into question and transcends many of the cognitive precepts that have shaped our collective view of the real and implied boundaries to physical space: while we are used to dynamic surfaces such as sails, ponds and lava flows, to be confronted by an impression of a surface that literally moves is extremely disconcerting.

It may have been a surprise to dECOi to win the competition, for suddenly the idea needed to be actualised. The wall's movement was then specified as generous; slight indentations and ripples were eschewed for great sweeping waves of up to half a metre of real-time displacement. This was effected by arrays of pneumatic pistons, the combined reflexive potential of which occurs in real time, and the control system processing the information from sensors calculates and signals to each piston a precise instruction at real-time speed: if you clap, the wall responds in sympathy and does not simply respond as a delayed reaction. Anything less risked trivialising the relationship between the wall and its environment: people were to be participants and not merely spectators.

Notes
1. 'Steiner's work falls into no stylistic category, its idiosyncrasies and originality make it as unique as the Czech phase of Rondo-Cubism.' Dennis Sharp, *Twentieth Century Architecture: A Visual History*, Lund Humphries (London), 1991, pp 46–7.
2. Eliel Saarinen, *The Search for Form in Art and Architecture*, Dover Publications (New York), 1948, original retitled and republished unabridged 1985.
3. Saarinen, op cit, p 41.
4. Ivan Massow, 'The Pillar of Shock Establishment has Proved It Can't Stand Dissent', *The Guardian*, Wednesday 6 February 2002.
5. Adrian Searle, 'Empty Promise', *The Guardian*, Tuesday 24 April 2001.
6. Saarinen, op cit, p 11.
7. J F Rafols, *Gaudí*, Editorial Canosa (Barcelona), 1929, p 201.
8. Mark Burry, *The Expiatory Church of the Sagrada Família*, Phaidon Press (London), 1993.
9. The studio ran both in the US and Australia during the whole of the first semester 2002. The

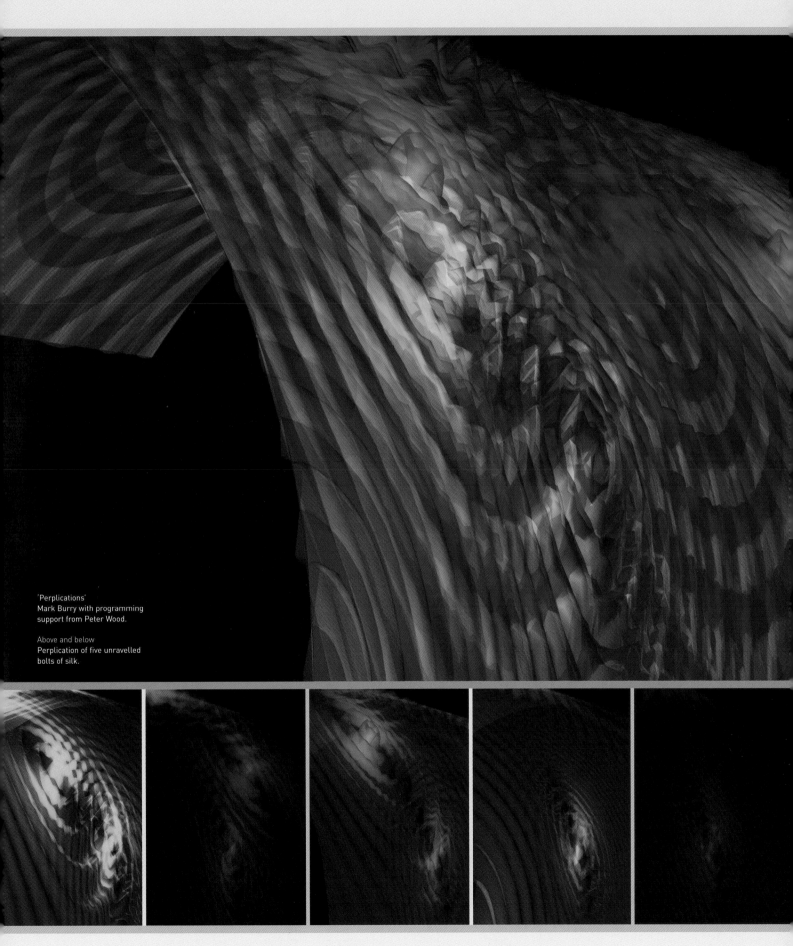

'Perplications'
Mark Burry with programming
support from Peter Wood.

Above and below
Perplication of five unravelled
bolts of silk.

projects were led by Jim Glymph and Dennis Sheldon (Gehry Partners), Bill Mitchell and Larry Sass (MIT), and Mark Burry and Grant Dunlop (RMIT).
10. An isoparm is an isoparametric curve of constant U or V value on a surface.
11. John Rajchman, *Constructions*, MIT Press (Cambridge, Mass), 1998, p 18.
12. Respectively, in terms of the roles played, Mark Goulthorpe, Alex Scott, Peter Wood, Mark Burry and Arnaud Descombes.
13. dECOi gathered a development team of engineers (ARUP), facade specialists (Spanwall), pneumatics engineers (Univer) and rubber research engineers (RAPRA), all of whom were obliged to take both their products and know-how to new extremes.
14. A prototype was inaugurated in March 2001 at the CeBIT Technology Fair in Hanover, which ran for six days.
15. 'Trauma, as we've noted, is not marked by an overfullness or excess of significance, but by an absence of conceptual registration. This suggests that the prefix hypo-, which is characterized by deficiency and lack, by a subliminal incapacity, might be more appropriate in considering the effect of such numerically-generated surfaces than hyper-, which denotes excess or extremity. Doubtless, since the terms are those of relative fullness or depletion, these should not be considered as exclusive oppositional terms ("expressivity" and "inexpressivity" will frequently cohabit according to context), but held in flux. But the Pallas house, which seems to numb its own expressivity – to engender a sort of inexpressive plasticity (which I've called on occasion an "Asiatic" sense), would seem to shift to the sublimity of hypo-surface. Aegis, then, as a surface of variable significance – a literal distortion of reference – would seem to carry this further, fluctuating between hypnosis and hallucination, the limit cases of optic sense. It will be interesting to gauge the resultant displacement of conceptual registration and to inquire as to the possibility of an emergent genre of hyposurface.' Mark Goulthorpe, 'Aegis Hyposurface: Autoplastic to Alloplastic', in Stephen Perrella (ed) 'Hypersurface Architecture II', *Architectural Design*, vol 69, no 9–10, 1999, p 65.
16. Saarinen, op cit, p 54.

The development of appropriate sensor, drive and control technology is a story in itself, but is not the issue here. Rather the issue is the challenge of developing a surface that is flat one moment (by moment we are talking of a few milliseconds) and alive with movement the next, pulses racing from one side to another at speeds of 60 kilometres an hour. Yet what material exists that can be taut, stretch up to half a metre out from a notional rest state, and snap back to being flat repeatedly over years of 'n' frames-a-second activity? For this reason, the surface was fractioned into small plates interconnected by rubber 'squids'.[13] The curved shape to the notionally triangular plates is occasioned by the geometry of movement, and is not simply an effect.

Critics and admirers alike have essentially formed their opinions through watching video footage of the wall at work rather than actually seeing it in use.[14] To an extent the project risks almost apocryphal reverence, similar to the Barcelona Pavilion by Mies van der Rohe perhaps, where the image was ultimately more profound in its influence than the short-lived progenitor. But with the Aegis Hyposurface, the image is nothing more than that: there is an inherent intellectual engagement if not compulsion within the experience of the wall that is not even hinted at, say, through video. The sensation of the air movement caused by the wall's mad fibrillations, the palpable shock of the pistons slamming home in certain instances, all hint at effects bordering on trauma, a synaesthetic transfer device.

After seeing video footage of the wall in use, one North American critic observed to me that it seemed to be 'male, and crudely instrumental'. Curious, then, that Goulthorpe named the hyposurface 'Aegis', the beguiling cloak of the glittering female warrior Athena, who deployed the Aegis as both cloaking device and weapon, alternately passive and aggressive, mute and significant. Ignoring the fact that this observation was made without the benefit of experiencing the wall 'live', it nevertheless calls into question how a mechanical contrivance might be anything other than crudely instrumental, let alone male? This observation provides a clue regarding some unique attributes that might otherwise be obscured through regarding the wall as a surface only, and not as a skin.

While skin, the organically physical confection of nature, is not easily replicated by mechanical engineers, we can at least replicate the reactive nature of the epidermis if we ignore the precise attributes of the subcutaneous tissue. In other words, the 'hypo' in Goulthorpe's neologistic hyposurface has many readings other than those that he as author of the term has supplied, and it would be as well to dwell not only on the compelling hypodermic 'depth' that allows such fluid movement but also on the 'hypo-mnesic digital brew' from which endlessly differential patterning evolves in time.[15] In the context of this paper, hypo can be the understatement of the effect that an inorganic skin can contribute to movement and perceptions of space. This is more than 'surface' alone, and the 'substance' of the contraption used to register such effects is somewhat less than the implications of digitally perceived and processed stimuli. The Aegis Hyposurface is completely contemporary in providing an amalgam of digital and physical tectonics to move beyond mere surface effects to that of promoting the fascination of skin and its relationship to body.

Concluding Comments

In the search for appropriate form for their buildings, architects have always been faced with at least two polar choices for a modus operandi whether designing a castle, cathedral, bicycle shed or a computer game. The first is whether or not to treat the formal appearance of their work as a personal signature. When more than one architect operates in this mode at the same time, we can argue that together they constitute an epoch of pluralism. However, at least since the Greeks established a cogent theory of architecture, a second choice for architects has been to work within a didactic construct. As an alternative to a pluralism of composition, most architects have consciously chosen to work in conformity to a given, and usually contemporary, architectural language or language revival. Eliel Saarinen's work is remarkable for its prescience if not its actual influence on work subsequently produced by his son, and also for its relevance today. His book, referred to earlier, was written to provide an account of the overriding insistence of the majority of Western architects to conform with stylistic protocols for at least two millennia, with only the occasional break-out such as Rococo being cited as a creative exception. He makes a plea for architecture to regain lost ground by returning as the 'mother' of the plastic and visual arts, having been supplanted by sculpture. The book is therefore a primer for an organic view of form.

But the habit of copying spread through the schools of architecture, and the art of building began gradually to lose its mother-place among the arts. Because of this, the strongest art-minds of the time became sculptors and painters, with the result that sculpture and painting gained prominent positions over the other arts – not least their former 'mother'. Sculptors and painters were

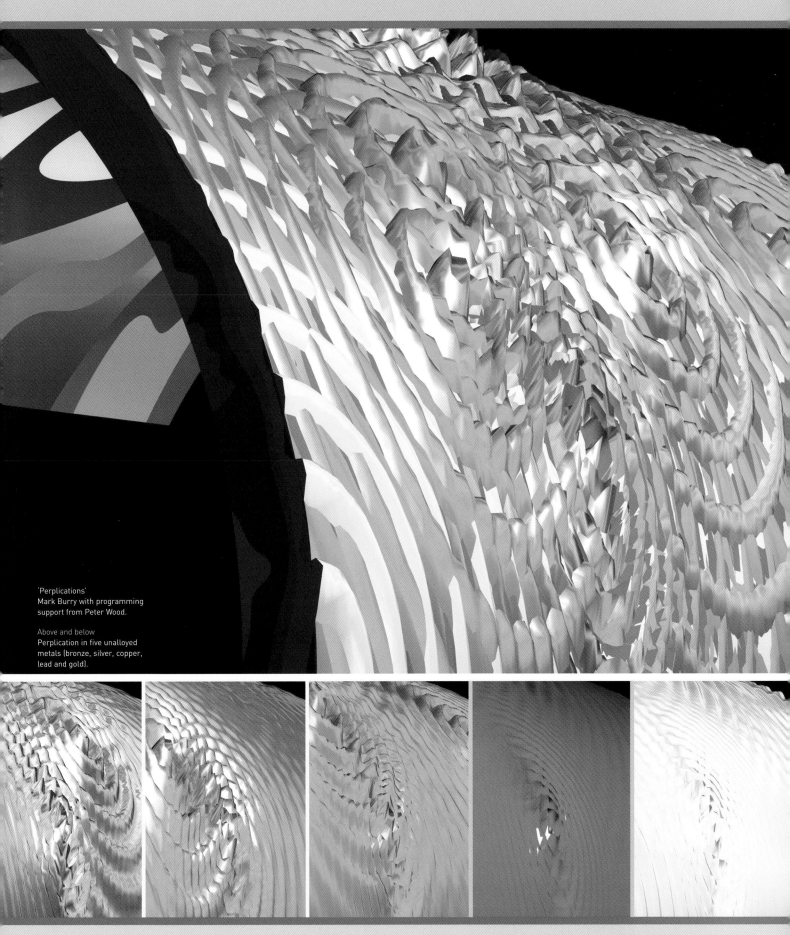

'Perplications'
Mark Burry with programming
support from Peter Wood.

Above and below
Perplication in five unalloyed
metals (bronze, silver, copper,
lead and gold).

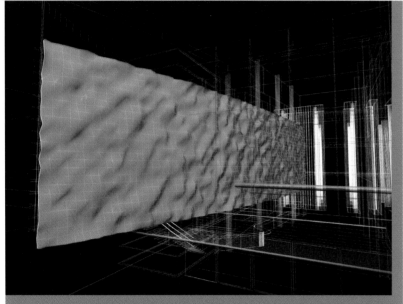

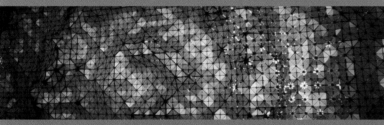

proud of these gained positions, and they
used them commandingly. Frequently the
building was looked upon as hardly more
than a suitable background for sculptural
and pictorial products, and it often
happened that sculptors and painters took
advantage of the building for the expression
of their artistic temperament.[16]

Whether 2000 years ago, 1948 or now, the
dilemma remains the same: to what extent
should we invent or otherwise obey the rules.
Probably the inventors have sponsored the
changes in the orthodoxy, but clearly deeper
cultural issues intervene in the development
of what we loosely define as 'style' – to a degree
it is the chicken-and-the-egg conundrum.
Within the question of whether to work
within or without an orthodoxy, or within a
style, architects face another dilemma: the

choice of whether to treat as an issue surface as the
interface between the eye and the constituent fabric
of form, or whether to ignore it. It is to those who
worry about the disruption that digital representations
cause to clear relationships between the surface of
artefacts and the materials used to form them that
this piece is dedicated. In particular, any debate on
the nature of form, its conception and its material
realisation becomes problematic as soon as virtual
representation issues are allowed to intrude. I have
contributed to this intrusion by outlining the proto-
digital scene set for me by Saarinen's influential
work published over half a century ago, providing the
context for the four cyber-real projects considered
critically in that light.

In terms of appearance and conformity with a style,
a Neoclassical composition can be represented as well
in ashlar masonry as it can in plaster render on brick.
Looking at Giulio Romano's work in Mantua, there are
many instances where stucco surfaces are
deteriorating, revealing the clumsier substrate beneath.
Two propositions are made here. The first is that in
this case, the Mannerist 'style' is concerned more
with effect than material reality, and it was the
representation of construction that was more important
to the architects of that time than the construction
giving actual voice to its formulation. Such architects
worked with equal motivation, it would seem,
regardless of the fact that stucco and stone employ
quite distinct skills in execution – the effect is more
important than the fact. This view is consistent with an
equivalent virtual representation of the same situation:
the dropped keystone, for example, tells the same story
whether in masonry, stuccoed brick or digital render.
How different this irrelevance or material voice is when
we contrast the brickwork of Kahn or Aalto at one
extreme with that of Gaudí and Sigurd Lewerentz at the
other, all of whom spoke clearly about their attitudes
to their use of materials through deed, if not in writing.

A second proposition is that regardless of motivation,
buildings deteriorate through attrition in the physical
world, and where economic constraints or lack of love
prevail buildings are inclined to ultimately reveal their
undergarments in this way. The poignancy of human
endeavour being challenged by forces of nature
exemplifies the human condition in a way that
challenges the digital realm. This is an obvious yet
nevertheless fundamental difference between virtual
and real representations of the world. In purely digital
craft, engagements with real forces are lost, the
challenges of nature bypassed. What new challenges
can we engage with as compensation for this reduction
in human artifice?

For the designer, mathematics has always had a role
to play, especially when descriptive geometry was the
essential means to communicate the complex whole into

Above
Aegis Hyposurface: physicality.

practically achievable elements. Traditionally it has intervened more in the description of surface than it has in the description of substance. Where today we regard our surfaces as geometrically derived (both Euclidean and non-Euclidean), we have difficulty in applying the same descriptive geometry principles to the design of the substance of any designed artefact with quite the same sense of purpose. Semi or completely automated construction component manufacture augmented by rapid prototyping detaches the hand from the design and making process. Mathematics, however, has the potential to re-engage the intellect with formal exposition in new and computationally assisted ways. The motivation for this piece has therefore been a search for equivalence in digital creativity in addressing real tectonic issues, not the relatively easy escape away from mundane terrestrial concerns into cyberspace.

This is the essential subplot to my account of the emerging contemporary relationships between surface and substance evidenced in a number of education- and practice-based projects that have a distinctly mathematical edge. Digital and real tectonics, when mathematically entwined, are the contemporary perplication that makes rubbish bag artwork seem anachronistic, with an intellectual content appearing to be little more than the contents of the piece itself: an artless surface with zero substance. Perplications are neither surface nor substance yet appear to be both at once, and represent what we can do today that could not be done so well before. ◬

The research reported here has been in part funded by the Australian Research Council. I acknowledge their support and that of the Junta Constructora of the Sagrada Família Church in Barcelona for the opportunities they provide for extending the work of Gaudí into contemporary architectural practice and research. Mark Goulthorpe of dECOi Architects is thanked for his generosity in providing the challenges and context for aspects of the work discussed here, as are Professor Keith Ball, Dr Alex Scott and Peter Wood for their mathematical and programming interventions explicit and implicit in much of the work reported on, and without whom it would not have been possible. Finally, colleagues and students at RMIT and MIT universities along with colleagues at Gehry Partners LLB are acknowledged for their commitment to parametric adventurism, the basis of some of the material in this piece.

Philibert De L'Orme Pavilion:

Towards an Associative Architecture

Architecture will only be widely conceived of as surface once automatised manufacturing techniques are successfully launched. These will allow for the abandonment not only of conventional additive design-and-construction processes but also the traditional distinction between ornament and structure. **Bernard Cache** discusses how his work at Objectile, developing assimilated software and hardware procedures for architects, has brought this evolution a step closer, as exemplified by his small-scale constructions such as the Philibert de L'Orme Pavilion.

Objectile's aim is to develop procedures, both software and hardware, that will make digital architecture a reality at an affordable cost for small architectural practices and the average consumer. After an initial series of experiments at the scale of objects, furniture and sculpture, Objectile developed a series of timber decorative panels that are basic building components. The firm now focuses on small-scale architecture where current state-of-the-art software is just starting to make it possible to contemplate a fully digital architecture.

The Semper Pavilion presented at Archilab (1999) in Orléans, France, was the first piece of digital architecture where everything from design procedures to manufacturing process was generated on the same software platform. Complex interlacings and undulating surfaces were algorithmically generated and then manufactured on a numerical command router right to the very last detail: for example the control of the tool path that creates texture on the surfaces. But such a small piece of architecture required two months' work for the office. Furthermore, were we to change the pavilion design, most of the operations would have to be repeated without significant time-saving.

Hence we have made the move towards fully associative design and manufacture, which for us appears to be the key issue for digital architecture. In an associative architecture, design procedures rely on a limited number of geometrical and numerical parents that can be easily modified and then regenerate the whole design of the building as well as its manufacturing programmes. In a small-scale architecture like the Philibert de L'Orme Pavilion (presented at Batimat 2001, in Paris), associativity means establishing a seamless set of relations between a few control points and the 765 machining programmes needed for manufacture on a numerical command router.

Due to the double-curvature cladding of a nonorthogonal structure, every single piece is different: the 12 structural elements, the 45 curved panels machined on both sides, and the 180 connecting pieces. Further, the need for automatic naming of the pieces became an issue. The following examines what were the state-of-the-art processes at the time of manufacture of this second pavilion, and explains why Objectile continues to focus on software development.

Projective Architectural Skeleton

The general architecture of the Philibert de L'Orme Pavilion is a projective cube, the three sets of ridges of which are arranged to converge in finite space. By moving these three vanishing points, the whole of the pavilion can be reconfigured down to the very last technical detail. In a similar manner to the way Philibert de L'Orme conceived his famous 'trompes' as a general system of two intersecting conical shapes,[1] this pavilion was designed as a homage to the inventor of stereotomy, which would eventually be systematised by another French architect, Girad Desargues.

It is very important to remember that projective geometry has implications much deeper than Brunelleschian representation, and that its fundamental concepts still remain to be integrated within computer-aided design (CAD) systems. As a result, we suggest the next generation of CAD software lies somewhere between 1550 and 1872.

Curvature

Just as a set of parallels is to be considered as a cone, the vertex of which is a vanishing point, so each wall of the pavilion was considered as a plane to be deformed into an ellipsoid tangent to the corresponding plane of the projective cube defined by its two vanishing points and centred on the third vanishing point. Because of the lack of projective geometry in current CAD software, such a procedure still needs to be implemented. When we designed the pavilion we drew an intuitive curve, but now we are close to a mathematical solution based on the principal sections of the ellipsoid. This involves intermediary constructions based on intersecting circles. For example, two circles might not always intersect as a figure in the real

plane, but always have two intersection points in complex space. Unfortunately, current CAD software does not enable us to take advantage of Poncelet's Principle of Continuity;[2] otherwise we would easily deform a standard cube with planar faces into a projective cube with curved faces. This is just one example of what we can expect from future projective CAD software.

Panelling

Each curved wall is divided by a 3 x 3 metre grid into nine panels using our software, which can deal with any type of dividing line. In this pavilion, they were curves resulting from the intersection of the curved surface of the walls with the four structural planes. Given the dividing lines and a series of 23 parameters, such as the width of the joints between panels or the diameter of the ball-nose tool, the abstract surface of the wall with no thickness is converted into the series of nine panels, each filed in a directory with a proper name and automatically oriented to the way it has to be positioned on the machine table.

One strong hypothesis of the Philibert de L'Orme Pavilion was that each wall was referred to the plane given by the corresponding face of the projective cube. This plane was to make things easier by providing a

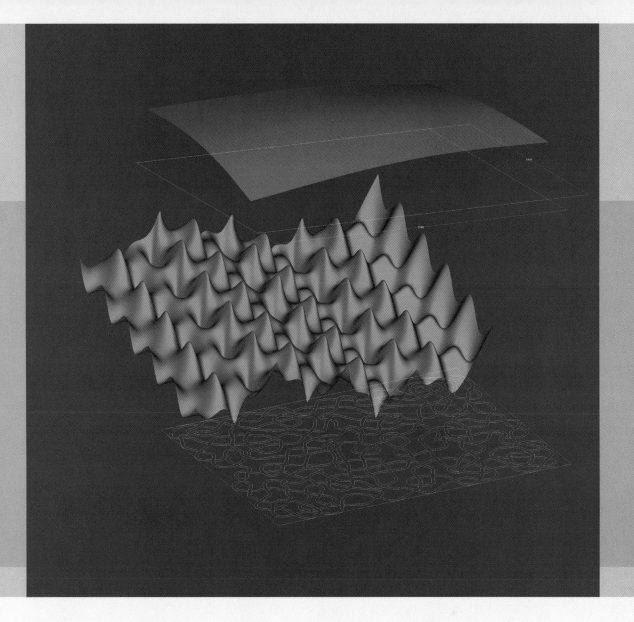

common reference to the machine table, the MDF boards, the assembly of the rough shape and its two counter shapes, the corner supports connecting the nine panels to the structure, and last but not least the orthogonal plane to the vertical tool of a three-axis router.

However, our software applications now enable us to do without this reference plane. Of course everything becomes more complex, but we are now able to automatically determine, for each of the panels, the plane that minimises the initial enclosing block of matter from which we start the machining operation. Not only do we minimise the matter needed, but we simplify all the manual operations required to prepare the rough shape. This is the way we conceive of digital architecture: we concentrate all the complexity in the software and the machining operations in order to make the manual operations fewer and more intuitive. Note that the two options of a common reference plane or a specific plane that minimises the enclosing block correspond to the two traditional techniques of stereotomy: *'la taille par équarissement'* and *'la taille par panneaux'*.

Interlacings

Another strong De L'Ormian feature of the pavilion is the interlacings carved into the panels on three of the walls and the roof. One need only pay a visit to the church Saint-Etienne du Mont, 100 metres behind the Pantheon in Paris, to be convinced that Philibert de L'Orme actually built there the most Semperian piece of architecture. Knots and interlacings have been a constant leitmotiv of this French Renaissance architect. Furthermore, if we consider the vocabulary of Desargues's Brouillon Project (1638), we can observe continuity between the French order of Philibert de L'Orme – a ringed tree trunk with knots and cut branches – and the basic concepts of the author of the mathematical treatise: trunks, knots, branches and foldings. Everything appears as if one of the most contemporary domains of topology (knots) were coiled into the very origin of projective geometry, anticipating the architectural geometry that would be presented by Felix Klein in his Erlanger Programm (1872).

A general knot theory is still lacking that would evidence the mathematical entity left invariant throughout the various configurations assumed by the same knot submitted to deformations. Nevertheless there exists a palette of techniques to generate knots on the basis of graphs. Objectile's application transforms these mathematical techniques into design

tools which, for instance, enable us to vary the thread thickness. We are aware of the fact that interlacing screens introduce an intermediary state between transparency and opacity and create the shallow-depth spaces experimented with in much traditional architecture, such as Islamic, and which continue to be examined by contemporary artists such as Brice Marden. If we accept the historians' position that the Modern Movement takes root in Laugier's writings, we could date the birth of modern architecture by a gesture of demolition: the destruction of the rood screen within the whitewashed cathedral of Amiens, a recommendation by none other than Laugier himself. Transparency is an old and essential myth of modern society that has taken new forms only with developments in information technology.

Panel-Machining Programs

Objectile's software applications are written in order to cope with surfaces with any type of curvature and without any process of standardisation, be these surfaces spheric, toric, swept or ruled, never mind triangulation. As a result, every single panel is to be machined with specific programs through a series of eight operations: contouring elements in boards; drilling the elements in order to establish a precise positioning of one element on top of the other with dowels; engraving them to prevent any mistake in assembly; surfacing the inner face of the panel; contouring the support at each corner of the panel; surfacing the outer face of the panel after turning it upside down; contouring the panel; and contouring the interlacings.

Manufacturing programs (G-code) must be absolutely error-free because they go directly from our computers in the office to the machine without any third-party control. Therefore they must be automatically generated. We are currently in the process of rewriting this software (to make the design and generate the G-code for objects that always vary), in order to refer each panel to the plane that will minimise the enclosing block. The series of operations will then be more complex because undercutting situations will have to be taken into account.

Structure and Connecting Pieces

Because the curvature of the panels is a general architectural problem that leads to a complex manufacturing process, we were aware that there was no other way to solve this than by writing our own software. Meanwhile, we largely underestimated the time needed to draw and generate the programs for the 12 structural elements and the 180 parts needed to connect the panels together and to the structure. Because of the projective geometry of the pavilion, each of these connecting pieces is different, and their geometry, although planar, has to be built between planes that make varying angles.

Once each of the pieces was drawn, they were held within an associative network of relations that made them dependent on the position of the three vanishing points. Moving any one of the three points would affect the whole geometry of the pavilion down to the very last elements, and their machining programs. We then made some progress in regard to the Semper Pavilion, achieving a first-level associativity. Once the project was finished we could then change it and produce a series of varying pavilions.

But it took us two months to design all 192 pieces, and the whole drawing process remained what we call 'a manual process' because we had to keep moving our mouse with our hand. Two months of detailing for an experimental pavilion is no big deal, but think of a real building. The design process in itself has to be automatised, and we cannot have a piece of software written for each type of design problem.

The solution consists in the logic of assembly and components, which creates a second level of associativity. Instead of drawing each single piece, we built up a component model which, again, lies upon a limited number of geometrical and numerical elements that we call 'pilots'. Once this model is worked out, we can create a component in the project by clicking its corresponding geometric pilots and fine-tuning its numerical parameters. But the component is not an isolated geometry; it can be said to be 'intelligent' because it carries with it a series of tools and processes that allows the component to interact with the surrounding parts and to generate their machining process.

Digital Architecture

What is digital architecture? Regarding the shape of buildings themselves, our answer is that we don't know. We have no clue about the future look for architecture and we very much question contemporary free forms when they become a cliché and sacrifice the past to the advantage of an absolute present. Marketing strategies are the new form of tyranny, and information technology can appear only as a *deus ex machina* if these strategies succeed in making us forget our own history. However, we hope that our explanations here will go some way towards the argument that digital technologies really put at stake the architecture of information lying behind the buildings, and that this architecture with digits also has to be designed. This is the task on which Objectile is currently focusing. ⟁

Notes
1. Philippe Potié, *Philibert De L'Orme: Figures du Projet*, Marseille, 1996.
2. Jean Victor Poncelet, *Traité des Propertiétés Projectives des Figures* (Paris), 1822.

Objectile, Philibert de L'Orme Pavilion (presented at Batimat 2001)

Background
Geometry of connecting pieces.

Inset left
Through view.

Inset right
Connecting piece.

In order to design surfaces that are both truly amorphous and irregular in their geometries, **Horst Kiechle** has had to write his own program, a rule-based generator or growth algorithm. He has taken this generative design technique through to construction, exploring the potential application of his system in his projects for the Darren Knight Gallery and Bambu restaurant in Sydney.

Amorphous

A couple entering Bambu restaurant:
'Hey, this is different – it's huge and it curves around behind the bar ...'
To the waiter: 'Yes, this table's fine, thank you.'
Orders placed – waiting for the entrées:
'This must be a sculpture – it doesn't line up in places and then it has these gaps. Maybe they had to cut it into slices to get it through the doors – or the segments are supposed to be sails like the Opera House ... look at it over there – it is such a cool building – this is a great table ...'
Meal finished, espresso, dinner partner returning from the bathroom: 'Ah, you are back – Did you like the large stone troughs as hand basins? Great idea! I just had a good look at this thing – it seems to be all made from triangles – I don't think any of them are the same – and there doesn't seem to be a system – if you follow these lines – they are all over the place: this one goes slightly up, continues in the next slice and bends down at that node. Then that line branches off and goes up to there ... I wonder what it's made of – can't be metal – it looks like it has bubbles here and there ... Yes, the espresso is good.'

In the accompanying scenario the couple gradually become aware of different surface characteristics of the restaurant space. Initially the surface shape is noted, as is the primary grid including the gaps between the segments. Subdivisions within a segment, which could be called a secondary grid or the finish of a surface, would generally only be noted if there is time for contemplation.

This illustrates two of Amorphous Constructions' main intentions: firstly to design and construct surfaces that are shaped freely in space ('amorphous' commonly means 'shapeless'); and secondly to avoid all repetition, self-similarity or regularity ('amorphous' as the technical term for solids such as glass or amorphous metals).

Standard design procedures are not really suitable for designing such amorphous structures. Traditional architectural drawing techniques – a set of three orthogonally placed drawing planes – strongly favour rectilinear designs. The most easily represented geometric surface entity in such a system is the rectangle; the most easily designed space consists of rectangles at right angles, resulting in the typical architectural box. Computer-aided architectural design software offers no real advantage as it is based on the

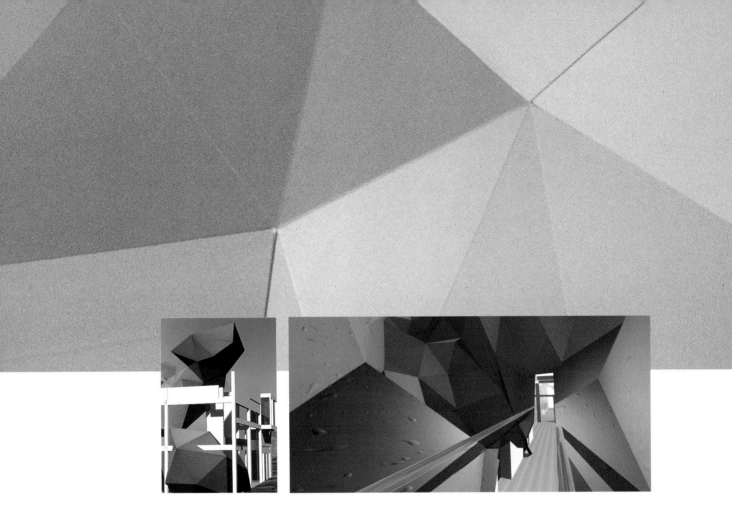

Structures

Above
Horst Kiechle, Darren Knight
Gallery project, Sydney, 1998.

Inset left
Horst Kiechle, Eisenman
Re-Visited project, retraced
images (Alias Power
Animator 4), 1995/96. View
of sculptural skin growing
through Eisenman's house.

Inset right
Horst Kiechle, Eisenman
Re-Visited project. View
inside sculptural growth.

same system simply transferred into the computer. Special-effects software for the film industry has the tools for free-form design but lacks the tools for construction. If one tries to combine the two, for example when designing with NURBS or Iso-surfaces, one has to convert them to polygonal surfaces for manufacturing purposes and this results in self-similar elements in a regular grid: even though each element might be unique, there are basically x elements along and y elements across the surface. Thus Amorphous Constructions developed its own software.

The Eisenman Re-Visited project, from 1995, was probably the most successful of the early attempts to generate alternative surface designs. Inspired by Eisenman's rule-based design approach for House II, I decided to write a rule-based shape generator (basically a growth algorithm). Instead of using rectangular volumes I worked with triangles. When viewing the resulting hybrid in virtual reality (VR) it seems to suggest that the 'grown' spaces generate a very different feel compared to the more familiar feel of the original spaces.

To experience such an amorphous space in reality I focused on construction and gave up the search for the magic algorithm or the all-new design tool. Instead I went back to the following basics:

- Three points in space define a planar triangle that can be cut from sheet material.
- Any curved surface can be approximated through triangular facets.
- Individual points are intuitively placed in 3-D space ideally in immersive VR, and define the polygons manually by connecting the points.

With this system and a bit of skill it would be possible to approximate a sphere, yet it would never have the precision or the regular subdivision of a sphere taken from the tool box of a CAD program. Amorphous Constructions welcomes this irregularity and imperfection, as for us it reflects the difference between natural and artificial things.

A series of low-budget full-scale gallery exhibitions enabled me to improve the design process and construction procedures. In designing these surfaces it is important to balance the average size of facets, which need to be small enough to approximate the

intended surface shape yet large enough to minimise the number of individual construction elements and thus the assembly budget. Once familiar with this process, there is a lot of creative potential in designing this secondary grid resulting from the joins between neighbouring facets. I believe that a subtle, if not subliminal, effect emanates from this patterning. Once aware of it, it provides stimulus to the eye, and is thus more satisfying than the regular grids, which are comprehended at a glance, yet continue to dominate our environments from floor tiling to suspended ceiling panels.

In the first gallery exhibition, stackable boxes with the amorphous space carved out of them supported the surface from behind. In subsequent gallery exhibitions, vertical columns with triangulated connector strips to the amorphous surface held up the walls and guaranteed the correct position. At Bambu, the individual segments are suspended from the ceiling. Rigidity within the segment was guaranteed through a very shallow tetrahedral reinforcement system (<120mm) that creates a spine along the length of the segment and tapers to material thickness along the edges. In a bid to break the visual solidity of the surfaces, I developed a frame system that provides the necessary structural strength while following and visually strengthening these irregular, secondary grid lines. Filler panels could now consist of slats, glass or even fabric.

Variations on a Theme: Comares Hall, Alhambra, Spain, explores the potential application of this system by replacing 700-year-old solid walls with a more contemporary surface-oriented design. To preserve one of the hall's most remarkable qualities – the perfect balance between a sense of spaciousness and shelter – the basic geometry of the 3-metre-thick walls with their almost room-deep window recesses has been copied. Rich ornamentation provides visual stimulus and veils the rectilinearity in the original space. In my remodelled versions the irregular faceting offers solutions somewhere between the visual overload of the original ornamentation and the straightforward barrenness of modernist lines. Whilst a gradual increase in transparency towards the window opening leads to an 'anthroposophic' softening, the inclusion of spiky elements results in a more energetic design within the framework of irregularity inherent in amorphous structures. Δ

Horst Kiechle acknowledges computer support through Sydney Vislab, manufacturing support through Visy Industries and the current fellowship by the Commonwealth Government through the New Media Fund of the Australia Council, its arts funding and advisory body. Horst Kiechle is represented by the Darren Knight Gallery, Sydney.

Opposite top
Horst Kiechle, Variations on a Theme: Comares Hall, Alhambra, Spain (variation 3: back view). Digital image of paper model, 2002.

Opposite middle and bottom
Screen capture of VRML models for Variations on a Theme: Comares Hall, Alhambra, 2002.

Above
Misho + Associates and Amorphous Constructions (Horst Kiechle), Bambu restaurant, Sydney, 2002. Kiechle and Misho + Associates worked on the initial design for the competition together. Once they had gained the commission, Kiechle was responsible for the design, construction and installation of the wall/ceiling and Misho + Associates designed and managed every other aspect of the restaurant's interior.

Right
Horst Kiechle, Darren Knight Gallery project, Sydney, 1998.

Surface-Talk

Until now our view of surface has been informed by the structure/ornament debate. For Vitruvius and most recently the modernists, the surface was an additional upper or outer layer extraneous to true tectonic structure, whereas for Gottfried Semper it was an ornamental textile supported by solid form. The use of digital design tools, however, has blurred the boundaries and rendered both camps' ideas redundant. For designers creating contiguous virtual and material surfaces it is no longer applicable to consider where architecture's tectonic origins lay in the temple or the tent. **Mark Taylor** proposes that the ideas of the philosopher Avrum Stroll could lead us to wholly new perceptions about surface as both a physical and an abstract entity.

Opposite
The surface of a lake generally
means the uppermost layer of
water: Waikoropupu Springs,
New Zealand.

Above left
A shadow has a boundary
and an edge but no surface:
Denton Corker Marshall (DCM),
Melbourne Museum, Australia,
2000.

Above right
We normally withhold surface-
talk from water that does not
lie smooth, such as when
gushing or spraying: Fountain,
Royal Exhibition Building,
Melbourne, Australia, 1897.

I am attracted to the philosopher Avrum Stroll's book *Surfaces*[1] because it offers the possibility of seeing surface as both a physical entity and an abstraction, and makes no claims about the primacy of one surface above another. It is a discussion that is played out on many levels and continuously returns to the topographic language of ordinary speech and the mathematics of geometry. Indeed the opening discussion uses ordinary things to pose extraordinary thoughts. For example, if a dice has six contiguous surfaces without gaps or openings, and it also has 12 edges, where are the edges? Can an edge be a surface? If a solid glass marble has a chip, is the chip in or on the surface? Does the chip have its own surface? These and many other everyday examples are used to pose the philosophical problem of perception through a discussion of how we define and perceive surfaces.

Stroll then examines the geometry of ordinary speech, including words like margins, limits, boundaries and edges, to draw similarities and differences between this topological language and the mathematics of geometry. In the same breath he manages to discuss surfaces as both abstractions and physical entities. At times I find the plausibility of arguments for surface as a theoretical abstraction neatly countered by equally powerful conceptions of surface based on everyday speech in the physical world.

In recent years many architects have used digital design tools to create complex nonorthogonal curvilinear forms and surfaces represented as either opaque or transparent spatial models. They reject the analytic geometry of Descartes and conventional Euclidean architectural language for one that embraces the world of the morphic, malleable and liquid. Some of these projects remain diagrammatic where surface is regarded as a two-dimensional programmatic field without thickness or bulk. Unconcerned by gravity, construction and traditional oppositional distinctions between surface and structure we might be prompted to ask what these seductively displayed surfaces are. Perhaps these experiments step outside the conventional structure/ornament debate to conceive form and surface as an 'immaterial and pliable two-dimensional datum with no depth or internal structure'.[2]

Other digital works are committed to material and constructional experimentation in an effort to realise form and surface as a new spatial condition. More closely linked to the tradition of architecture they are concerned with the physical base of surface, and its articulation as a necessary condition for the material practice of architecture. One model regards surface as an abstraction, the other as physical. Though they seem to be in opposition, both models have an equally sound theoretical base, and are closely allied to the two models of surface put forward by Stroll.

To appreciate Stroll's work and its relevance to architecture necessitates engaging with different conceptions of surface than that used in traditional

architectural practice. When reading histories and theories of architecture we find many positions founded on Vitruvius and Alberti use bodily metaphors and gender characteristics to describe transcendent metaphors of architecture. We are assured that clothing, cladding, skin and bones portray various states of dressing and undressing surface from structure. And in the search for authority Alberti placed the origin of architecture as being constructed naked and later dressed with ornament, whereas Gottfried Semper transformed this account into one in which architecture began with the placement of textile ornament, followed by solid structure.

In the former, surface is seen to be a resultant condition, one in which sur-face as an 'upper' or 'outer' layer is able to be scraped back, thereby revealing the true, inner architectural surface. Under this conception surface is generally assumed to have thickness which covers and masks. This is a familiar position that enables the elevation of structure (as masculine), and the concomitant devaluation of surface decoration and ornament (as feminine). While Gottfried Semper reverses this relation, theory still maintains an oppositional dualism of surface and structure. In either case,

a conceptual distinction is made between the outer covering, cladding or skin and the inner structural and gravity-bearing elements, but always one is privileged above the other. Moreover, the short step to declaring that something that is enclosed (enclosed by cladding) is 'hidden' arises because a thing is not 'outwardly visible'. However, we can imagine the inner and outer surfaces of a transparent hollow cube being clearly visible if inaccessible.[3]

The beauty of Stroll's text is that he privileges neither the outer cladding nor the inner substrate as primary – they are simply different parts of a nonhomogeneous entity. Admittedly his concern is with the perception of these objects, not their authority. Likewise my concern is not with originary foundations to architecture but our perception of architecture through surfaces. Certainly Stroll makes a distinction between a solid homogeneous object in which the outer surface is the same as the inner material, and a covered object in which the inner material is different to the outer mantle. The former, such as the simple steel ball or marble, has consistent materiality, whereas the latter includes both baseballs and the more complicated case of the earth. Here Stroll observes that some things, such as lakes and forests, cover the surface of the earth, and other things such as lava are not foreign matter and therefore not new matter. He notes that an outer covering may consist

of a hard protective layer encasing a soft liquid centre, or a soft covering to a hard inner substrate. Neither is privileged as supporting the other – neither is primary.

Stroll probes surface relative to depth by working through a number of physical examples from dice, glass marbles, lakes and tables, through to molecular surfaces. He shifts between a Leonardo da Vinci conception of surface as abstraction to a scientific molecular model, and reveals two, possibly four, conceptions of surface. Firstly he discusses the Leonardo (LS) conception, which considers surface as an interface, a common boundary without divisible bulk that does not belong to either of the contiguous entities that are in contact. Surface is seen as an abstract entity that marks the theoretical distinction between two things, or thing and nothingness. Catching our imagination he proffers an example of the latter – an asteroid in space where the outer limit of the asteroid divides it from the vacuum.

A second conception of surface as an abstraction concerns the surface that belongs to its corresponding entity, what Stroll calls the DS surface. This surface is found by progressively thinning out a physical surface

until it is no longer a physical part but is a conceptual limit, a boundary – the upper limit. It is still the object's surface, and is equally applicable to the asteroid in a vacuum, even though it does not separate the asteroid from anything. Under this model, surface is a thin transparent film and like the LS model has no divisible bulk. Returning to ordinary language Stroll suggests the surface of a flat lake could be found by progressively thinning the physical water until it is no longer a thing but is a boundary. The surface of the lake is generally understood to be the upper part where air meets water and not the lower part where water meets bedrock, which itself is another surface. In part this is based on everyday language, which generally refers to the surface of the lake as the upper layer.

As against these abstract surfaces, Stroll counterpoises two other conceptions of surface that are treated as physical; the ordinary person's observation (OS) and the scientific view put forward by G A Somorjai (SS). Both concepts depend on surfaces having physical properties that include depth or divisible bulk. The OS is the surface of the entity and is a part of the object (usually the upper or outer part) deep enough to become marked, scratched or scuffed. It has thickness and is also a boundary. In some cases these surfaces may be outer coverings such as mantles, or be the outward limit of a homogeneous

material like glass, steel or stone. And as stated earlier, the mantle may or may not be structural. Some outer coverings may be thin coats of paint that can be sanded back to reveal an original surface; others, such as the covering to a golf ball, are more complex as there is no 'original' surface beneath the covering. However, with the latter the outer mantle does mask or hide the inner substrate.

Lastly, the SS surface is conceived physically as the last layer of atoms, the uppermost aspect of an object. Like the DS model it is conceived as the progressive thinning of a material, moving from the centre to the boundary until the last thin layer of atoms is reached. It is 'the last layer that belongs to that object before one moves into a medium of a different sort'.[4] Using an electron microscope, Somorjai photographs 'clean' deposit-free surfaces that are one atom thick, a surface that is found to be heterogeneous rather than homogeneous. It contains a number of topological features such as terraces, steps and kink atoms, which Somorjai describes as a 'system'. It is not unlike a hillside landscape composed of bumps, pits and raised areas, with

a number of six-sided adatoms that resemble ivory cubes. It is important to remember that in the ordinary world we cannot see these features with the naked eye, neither can we see small microscopic blemishes, cuts and marks on the surface. Although this conception is based on scientific observation, we can say that in a Deleuzian sense we reach a moment when the entity 'becomes' surface. That is, becoming surface occurs at a molecular level as well as at a molar level.

All four of Stroll's conceptions treat surface as a boundary, which is not the same as saying all boundaries are surfaces. For example, Stroll notes that a shadow has a boundary but no surface. Other objects that he attributes as having no surfaces include gushing water, clouds, trees and humans. He suggests that humans do not have surfaces 'but a person's skin has a surface'.[5] We can touch our skin but this is not the same as touching our surface. Skin can have a surface but any operations performed are usually performed on skin rather than surface. In part this distinction is made because of human mobility and lack of rigid boundaries – after all, what is our shape? For the ordinary person skin is a boundary but not a surface, whereas for Somorjai science would declare it a surface in a molecular or atomic sense.

Notes
1. Avrum Stroll, *Surfaces*,
University of Minnesota Press
(Minneapolis), 1988.
2. Johan Bettun, 'Skin deep:
polymer composite materials
in architecture', in Ali Rahim
(ed) 'Contemporary Techniques
in Architecture', *Architectural
Design*, Vol 72, 2002, p 76.
3. Stroll, op cit, p 91.
4. Stroll, op cit, p 54.
5. Stroll, op cit, p 75.
6. Had the human figure been
laid out in a foetal position the
geometric outcome may have
been very different.
7. Leon Battista Alberti, *On the
Art of Building in Ten Books*,
trans Joeseph Rykwert, Neil
Leach and Robert Travenor, MIT
Press (Cambridge, Mass), 1988,
p 69.
8. Mark Wigley, *White Walls,
Designer Dresses: The
Fashioning of Modern
Architecture*, MIT Press
(Cambridge, Mass), 1995, p 25.
9. Gottfried Semper, *The Four
Elements of Architecture and
Other Writings*, trans Harry
Malgrave and Wolfgang
Herrmann, Cambridge
University Press (Cambridge),
1989, p 24.
10. Ibid., p 254.

Given these two (possibly four) conceptions of surface, and Stroll's reluctance to accept that humans have surface, two thoughts emerge regarding the traditional mapping of the human body onto architecture; a mapping that equates structure with bones, and cladding with skin. Firstly, what we regard as an architectural skin might not be a surface (in a Stroll sense), although it might have surface properties; and secondly, the traditional metaphor might be too exclusive to be of real value in our understanding of architectural surfaces and the overturning of binary divisions.

The traditional mapping of the nonrigid animate human body onto architecture was enacted as a means of determining proportion and geometrical relationships for a rigid inanimate object. What should be noted is that in the particular laying-out of the Vitruvian man to determine rules of measurement, the animate human was made rigid – much like a statue or a corpse, both of which Stroll suggests can be discussed relative to surface conditions, whereas the human cannot.[6]

What is clear from Stroll's work is that surfaces need to be discussed relative to the operations performed on them – painting, carving and finishing – as well as the materials we use to perform these operations. For example, a surface (water) can be rippled, the substrate beneath the surface (more water) cannot be rippled. Further, if we remove the condition of architecture having a mythical truth between structure and cladding then a much more interesting understanding of surface is possible.

Alberti's thin surfaces that act as a covering or cladding to an underlying substrate have a similar conceptual base to Stroll's OS surface. Here substrate structures such as 'solid' walls are the architectural surface on which an artificial ornamented surface may be placed, and the substrate wall is regarded as a 'true' original surface that is covered or masked. However, in his description of wall construction, Alberti maintains that good practice dictates that walls are composed of 'infill and twin skins or shells on either side'.[7] That is, the 'true' substrate structure is itself composed of an outer mantle (the outer skins of similar or different stone) and an inner substrate (rubble). This is a hard outer mantle to a soft inner substrate. In which case plaster (modified stone) and paint are further coverings to a layered non-homogeneous entity. Compositionally the wall comprises a soft inner material protected by a harder outer layer, covered by a softer finishing layer (which may or may not be ornamented) – a laminated mantle.

Similarly, the Semperian model of architecture as cladding/clothing supported by a nonhomogeneous substrate can also be examined this way and found to be a similar entity. Locating architecture as a textile art in which seamed-together textile walls envelop and wrap to give spatial enclosure, Semper suggests that architecture 'turns out to be nothing more than texture'.[8] So irrespective of whether the argument concerns clothing or cladding, true or artificial surfaces, the discussion is primarily about 'texture' – a surface characteristic. Indeed, Semper argued that the figures chiselled into the gypsum of Assyrian alabaster bas-reliefs imitated the style of the textile dressing;[9] like other surface markings they are scratched and deepened into the surface.

As well as recognising the physical qualities of wall surfaces and the necessity for solid walls, Semper also notes that the woven surface was first conceived as a means to separate inner life from outer life and concerns the formal creation of the idea of space. That is, the wall that secures spatial enclosure has 'nothing directly to do with space and the division of space'.[10] Semper further suggests that this conception of surface as abstraction precedes the wall as physical entity, a judgement not made by Stroll. ⌂

VOLCANIC
The Architecture
Whakaari/

Sarah Treadwell explores the notions of surface and spatial instability in a volcanic terrain. On the crater's edge, notions of substance and vapour, and foundational strategies of stable ground dissipate into flames. She imagines the persistent effects of such an elusive and yet very material landscape on architectural and filmic sensibilities.

MATTER:
of
White Island

Volcanic ash thickens the air and the ground, as lava flows. Pumice rocks float and gravity explosively reverses. 'Maybe it is not the destructiveness of the volcano that pleases most, though everyone loves a conflagration, but its defiance of the law of gravity to which every inorganic mass is subject.'[1] Not neutral or comprehensible but atmospheric and catastrophic, volcanic passage is characterised by a disruptive spacing apart. Architectural atmosphere, Mark Wigley argues, seems to start where construction stops, but as he points out atmosphere is also produced by physical form.[2] While volcanic effects of explosion, layering and steamy coagulation may be seen as an undoing

mobile, doubling between the fictive and the occupied, emulating the already mobile geology that refuses to maintain boundaries as inevitable or stationary.

Successive populations of New Zealand have tended to be premised on mobility, subject to pressure. Travelling from provisional stabilities of previous homes, rejecting stasis and natal foundations, 19th-century immigrants from Great Britain were flung to the edge and limits of inhabitation, perilously close to the ends of the earth. They encountered a volcanic shaping of land that harboured the possibility of interiority even as it violently repelled settlement. This image of tumultuous occupation persists in reinventions of Aotearoa/New Zealand; foundational difficulties, valorisation of structure and a statistically recorded

WHITE ISLAND, IN THE BAY OF PLENTY.

of architecture, such effects are also the constructional matter of architectural space in Aotearoa/New Zealand, three islands in the South Pacific named after a long white cloud.

Peter Jackson's film *The Lord of the Rings: Fellowship of the Ring* (2001) continued a tradition of fashioning Aotearoa/New Zealand and its landscape around a central image of a smouldering volcano. Mount Doom (familiar to locals as Mount Ngauruhoe), a rounded symmetrical cone, stereotypically volcanic, brooded over a vast army of strange creatures swarming across the high desert plane of Middle Earth/New Zealand. Geography had become

tendency to domestic violence all colour architecture in these islands.

Nicholas Reid has pointed out that the

New Zealand seen on the screen ... seems to consist exclusively of high exploding volcanoes, blood-red skies, rivers of lava and earthquakes. It isn't much like the country we live in. But then surely they wouldn't get something like that wrong in a real film? Maybe New Zealand genuinely is the way the film shows it – only we haven't noticed it before.[3]

Screening New Zealand as a volcanic effect is to be expected in a country that Francis Pound described as being productively invented as 'three high heaps of earth discovered in the blue of a desolate sea'.[4]

In colonial accounts, after 170 days at sea travellers from England would encounter a volcanic precursor, a heightened detail or a saturated condition of the generally volcanic islands of New Zealand. They saw, unexpectedly, the white steam of Whakaari/White Island, a small active volcanic island smouldering 49 kilometres north of Whakatane in the Bay of Plenty. Clouds of volcanic steam and smoke that continue to issue from White Island repeat, with a twist, the long white cloud of Aotearoa/New Zealand. Part of a volcanic zone that lies between an area of elevation and one of

missionaries it was, in the engraving, depicted as wasted and insubstantial (a thinness that reoccurs in subsequent theatrical constructions of the island as a film set). The core matter of foundational security has been swallowed in this evocation of the diabolical. In the image, three figures in a small canoe bend their backs in an effort to paddle away from the steaming crater. The engraving is an apocalyptic depiction of malevolent emptiness that prophetically reflects the rising sea levels of the Pacific region.

Colonial painter Charles Heaphy (1820–81) centred a watercolour on the crater of Whakaari/White Island (c1850).[6] The painting depicts four figures within the volcanic interior. Two cloaked Maori men, in the foreground of the image, gesture towards two European

depression, Whakaari/White Island, on an axis of upheaval, prefigures the shaky foundations and violent history of colonial attempts at settlement.

Missionary Reverend Richard Taylor (1805?–73) in *Te Ika a Maui: or New Zealand and its Inhabitants* (1870), included an engraving based on his own ink sketch of Whakaari/White Island as a thin crust wrapped like a cloak around a steaming, gaping hole. The emaciated wrap of land could not disguise its vacant interior or the impossibility of containment. From the emptiness at the heart of the engraving issue threads of wispy steam. If the land was held to be fruitful territory for

men who are about to test the bearing capacity of the (middle) ground. The Europeans hold large boulders high in the air and look towards the variable edge between land and liquid in a foundational gesture that seeks to secure firm footing upon which subsequent architecture might depend. Will the hurled rocks activate a response from ground imagined by 19th-century writers as 'mother earth', a maternal *chora* that received impressions but cast no formal effects? Small footprints impress tracks across the dun-coloured surface; ground is pictured as unreliable in both its softness and mobility.

There is an odd sense of failed communication in the image; do the Maori seek to warn the Europeans of

Notes
1. Susan Sontag, *The Volcano Lover: A Romance*, Harper Collins Canada (Canada), 1992, p 32.
2. Mark Wigley, 'The architecture of atmosphere', *Daidalos*, 68, 1998, p 18.
3. Nicholas Reid, *A Decade of New Zealand Film: Sleeping Dogs to Come a Hot Friday*, John McIndoe (Dunedin), 1986, p 9.
4. Francis Pound, 'Distance looks our way', in Mary Bar (ed) *Distance Looks Our Way: 10 Artists from New Zealand*, The Trustees, Distance Looks Our Way trust (Wellington, New Zealand), 1992, p 28.
5. Richard Taylor, *Te Ika a Maui: or New Zealand and its Inhabitants*, William Macintosh (London), 1870.
6. Charles Heaphy, *Whakari or White Island; view of the crater looking northwest from crater margin*, c1850, watercolour, 393 x 605 mm, Ref No C-025-018, Alexander Turnbull Library, Wellington, New Zealand.
7. Vicki Kirby, *Telling Flesh: The Substance of the Corporeal*, Routledge (New York and London), 1997, p 5.
8. Laurence Simmons, 'Distance looks our way: imagining New Zealand on film', in Deb Verhoeven (ed) *Twin Peeks: Australian and New Zealand Feature Films*, Damned Publishing (Melbourne), 1999, p 41.
9. New Zealand Publicity Office, *Portals of the Underworld*, 1930.
10. *Under the Southern Cross/The Devil's Pit*, Universal, USA, 1929. Directed by Alexander Markey & Lew Collins. Photographed by Wilfred Cline.
11. *The Seekers (aka Land of Fury)*, UK, 1954. Directed by Ken Annakin. Produced by George H Brown. Based on a novel by John Guthrie.
12. *Strata*, Phase Three Films, 1982. Directed by Geoff Steven. Produced by John Maynard. Photography by Leon Narby.
13. Toni Morrison, *Playing in the Dark: Whiteness and the Literary Imagination*, Harvard University Press (Cambridge, Mass), 1992, p 33.
14. Sontag, op cit, p 113.
15. WT Parham, *Island Volcano: White Island New Zealand*, William Collins (Auckland), 1973, p 61.

Opposite
Craig Potton, 'White Island. Crater Edge'.

some impending danger? There is no perceptible response from the men about to throw the rocks, who may not hear the words through the mutters and hissing of an eloquent ground. Vicky Kirby, writing of the complications of the nature/culture divide, posits an 'alien within – in the form of a very real possibility that the body of the world is articulate and uncannily thoughtful'.[7] Rather than seeing the material world as the substance to which discourse gives form or a dissembling construct – a 'reality effect' – she argues for an enmeshing of materiality and ideality.

Sulphuric fumes from Whakaari/White Island (a diabolical whiff of chemical matter) etch their way into national imagery in a succession of volcanic films located in New Zealand. According to Laurence Simmons, in such films '[g]eological evolution is collapsed into the history of colonisation and it seems that nation, history, rock and soil are all products of a single fantastic eruption'.[8] Not only is the narrative force of eruption encountered and utilised in the Whakaari/White Island films but also the architectural effects of its filmic deployment as a precursor to, or an intimation of, commotion. Frequently depicted at the beginning of movies the island volcano operates as a gate to spatial conditions that are habitually inaccessible or censored.

Films that picture Whakaari/White Island, include *Portals of the Underworld* (1930),[9] *Under the Southern Cross* (1929),[10] *The Seekers (aka Land of Fury)* (1954)[11] and *Strata* (1982).[12] All have a tendency to allude to the diabolical nature of the island, composing it as a serpent's pit, a dragon's or devil's pit, and an island of fury; terms for legendary creatures, mythical spaces. In particular, *Portals of the Underworld*, a documentary about Whakaari/White Island made by the New Zealand Government Publicity Office, activated notions of an underworld. The film starts with an image of a boat approaching the island and the caption: 'Into "THE GATES OF HELL" – the well-named landing place on White Island is on the edge of a steam-torn crater'. The uncertainty of arrival is escalated into peril by the crater; partial, unreliable, torn apart by steam. Nineteenth-century missionaries often saw their passage to New Zealand as an approach to the abyss of darkness. Exposed in the crater, the shaded classical underworld became aligned to a Christian hell.

The portals referred to in *Portals of the Underworld* are an entry point to be negotiated, a partitioning between the volcanic and the mythic. Eurydice was immured in the shade of the underworld because of a glance by Orpheus. In her journey back to the land of the living and light she was petrified by a backward stare into the depths. A parallel sequence in the Whakaari/White Island movie depicts a man running out of the frame, which then clouds over. When the steam clears a petrified figure appears, a geological formation known as 'Lot's Wife'. Volcanic petrification is associated with partial or backward vision and, biblically, with the destruction of architecture.

Bursts of vapour issuing from crevices and cracks in the ground, carefully recorded on film, constitute evidence of a subterranean force that operates with the half-seen and the half-known. Steam on Whakaari/White Island constructs an elusive labyrinth that also touches everything; white steam as miasma penetrating all surfaces and crevices. In a much later New Zealand film, *Strata* (1982), steam is used as both contaminant and purifier. *Strata* starts on Whakaari/White Island with a volcanologist and a photographer, isolated from the atmosphere by protective clothing, moving in and out of rising, billowing steam. The men become partial, fragmentary and unexpectedly vivid in detail. Whakaari/White Island in this manifestation is veiled and unearthly, a concealed whiteness that seems 'to function as both antidote for and meditation on the shadow that is companion to this whiteness'.[13]

Surface Occupation

Attempts have been made to exploit and occupy White Island despite its acid air, shifty ground and unpredictable eruptions. Various owners of the island mined the sulphur and minerals that coloured the island with glittering hues. New Zealand Manure and Chemical Company (1883) was followed by White Island Sulphur Company (1913), White Island Agricultural Chemical Company (1925) and White Island Products (1927). Along with the short-lived golden prospects of the sulphur and fertiliser industries, precious stones were imagined. White Island was seen as a repository of treasure and the attempts to mine its fictional wealth seem to connect it functionally with the 'ground where the dead live, stacked in layers ... the mineral level of existence'.[14]

Traces of the marginal architecture that accommodated mining still remain on the island though the earliest buildings disappeared cataclysmically. The first settlement, which included a boiler house, retort house, cookhouse/dining room and the men's accommodation, was situated within the crater. During the night of 10 September 1914, thermal and seismic activity leading to ground collapse caused a lahar (mud flow) that swept all the buildings in the crater out to sea. Ten men were killed. A second factory was built in 1928–30 and used ferroconcrete in an attempt at

Top
Craig Potton, 'White Island. Crater Edge'.

Middle
Craig Potton, 'White Island. Steam'.

Bottom
Craig Potton, 'White Island. Surface'.

permanence, although it was uncertain what the acidic air would do to the materials.

After the destruction of the first huts, a new camp for the workers was established outside the crater (c1925) using second-hand railway accommodation. 'These were each eleven feet by ten, and were joined together to provide a range of bedrooms. There was the further advantage that, being of sectional construction, these were convenient for shipping'.[15] Domesticity was forced into small timber structures premised on movement. The history of building on Whakaari/White Island is of temporary structures, dangerous dwellings and annihilation in the night. It is also a history of material failure. The atmosphere of the island corrodes and corrupts; metals are eaten, objects fall apart. There is no pure water and the first purification plant corroded.

Domesticity
Nevertheless, the landscape has been represented as occupiable. It was recorded that on one occasion when the island was operating as a film set local actors slept on the volcanically warmed beach without covers. The volcanic, fiery warming and warning of the world does not entirely deny a surface condition of occupation. Rather the volcanic becomes a metaphoric evocation of an impossible interior that both sustains and represses violence. Bubbles of air within a lava flow make pockets that solidify, forming caves. Within the flow of uncontrollable matter, space opens and interior conditions coalesce.

In *Under the Southern Cross*, lava caves on Whakaari/White Island become a site of illicit union that ultimately leads to conflict and death. A fight, which starts in a lava cave, ends in a hand-to-hand struggle on the rim of the volcano. The crater edge, situated between substance and vapour, is a line on which the volcanic depends, exploiting the shifting boundary between matter and nonexistence and rendering precarious distinctions between interiority and exteriority. White steam billows high above two small black figures; one man is eventually thrown into the steaming crater.

In *The Seekers*, treachery and war are accompanied by shots of Whakaari/White Island's volcanic field. Death occurs amidst steam and mist, volcanic heaving of earth and mud. An attack on a colonists' settlement takes place in the enclosure of a black night and the dark interior of a settler's log house is shown as it progressively burns. The English heroine and hero finally die on the flaming roof. The house itself becomes volcanic as its interior, in which birth, family life and repression were located, spews into the sky. It is the difficult, marginal interior that provides a fiery thread linking these White Island films. In *Under the Southern Cross*, interiority only prevails in volcanic conditions where it is always at risk. In *The Seekers*, the dark family interior dissipates in flames and in *Strata* the darkness of a hut in the bush perpetuates close associations between femininity, violence and interiority.

In Aotearoa/New Zealand foundational security, bodily unity and material permanence become showered with ashes of burning structure, scored with anxieties about colonial occupation and ornamented with anticipated illumination. Architectural constructions in New Zealand depend upon foundations that are fiery and unreliable, constructing domesticity as volatile, transitory and violent. Yet pungent sulphuric odours, thickened atmosphere and fluid volcanic matter still retain the potential to heat the chill propriety of colonial fabrications. Volcanic architecture, risky and threatening, underlies the warm and tumultuous possibilities of island-dwelling on the edge of the world. ⌀

Thanks to ArchDrc 401 and MRA for their comments and suggestions.

Masked Matter and Other Diagrams

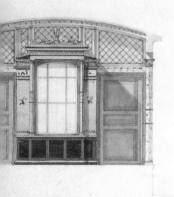

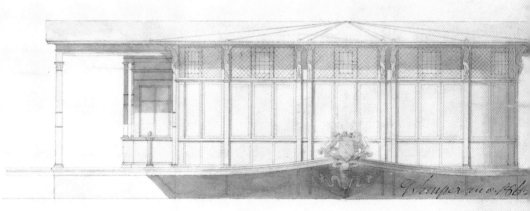

In architecture the primacy given to technical innovations has meant that new surface treatments have entailed little more than the current highest-tech clothing. **Hans Frei** describes how Gottfried Semper, Donald Judd and Herzog & de Meuron all present alternative approaches that place the emphasis on the creative transformation of technical conditions into new architectural concepts of the surface – their point of departure being the special reality of matter, whether this be the mask or the diagram.

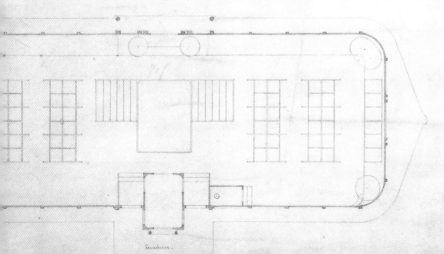

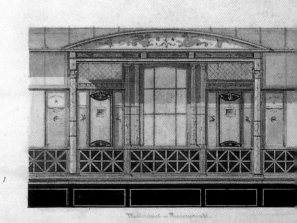

Mediaisation, immaterialisation, digitalisation are aspects of a new materialism that will suck off the last bit of substance clinging to architectural surfaces. Nonetheless, for effects and achievement capability they top everything that up to now seemed possible. In this context one speaks less of facades and more often of skin or, more neutrally, of sheaths and surfaces.

What is New?
Since architecture is closely related to the technical disciplines, it is not a great leap to identifying that which is new in architecture with technical innovations. Technical progress would, however, be misunderstood if a new architecture were expected from every technical innovation. In T*he Question Concerning Technology*, Martin Heidegger describes the essence of the technical as an act through which man reveals nature and puts it to his own uses. As a rule, technical innovations are nothing other than sophisticated variants of the game of concealing and revealing.[1] However extreme they might be from a technical point of view, they always follow the same principle of putting something to service. Thus the most intelligent facades, the most translucent veils and the most interactive

media facades are not fundamentally different from a classical facade. These are filters, dividing de facto two sides from each other while simultaneously connecting them somehow on a representational level – half showing their own constructedness and half what lies behind it.

Precisely because the technical plays such a dominant role in Western architecture it is nearly impossible to liberate architectural surfaces from the culture of representation. As opposed to this, in their considerations and works Semper, Judd, and Herzog & de Meuron present other approaches to the utilisation of technical innovations. To them, the application of technical know-how is less important than the creative transformation of technical conditions into new architectural concepts of the surface. In order to achieve a surface beyond representation, they make their point of departure the special reality of architecture and don't stop with merely fitting it with a new (technical) set of clothing.

Masked Matter
Gottfried Semper's textile theory can be seen as a first step towards the nonrepresentational architectural surface. The point of departure for this theory was the discovery of the coloured setting of classical temples. Although this issue had been intensely discussed prior

to Semper's time, only Roman examples were debated, never the white marble glory of the Greek temple. That is until Semper himself examined the Theseus temple in Athens and here, too, found the remains of colour. From this, Semper deducted that the Greeks only built their temples out of marble because marble provided a good base for paint. Clothing or masking thus became for Semper the first principle of architecture. He regarded a masonry wall somewhat like a clothed wall, and formulated this view provocatively in a footnote in *Der Stil*:

> To put it in modern terms, every artistic creation, on the one hand; every artistic pleasure, on the other, is predicated by a certain carnival mood. The carnival candle's glow is the true artistic atmosphere. Destruction of reality – matter – is necessary where form as a meaningful symbol, as an independent creation of man should come to the fore. The means employed for the artistic impression intended should be erased and they should not step out of character in notable misery. The unspoiled feeling in all earlier artistic attempts made by primitive peoples leads to this conclusion. All the great masters

in all fields of art returned to this fact only that these in eras of a higher artistic development were also masking the matter of the masks.[2]

What Semper vehemently attacks here is the short circuit in thought between matter and the meaningfulness of a building such as was typical of the thinking of the then fashionable classicists. For example, Carl Bötticher read the structure of a temple – the tectonic – as a kind of grammatical deep structure from which philologists would be able to decode the meaningfulness of a building.[3] It was precisely this idea that Semper opposed. The destruction of matter – justified by the practice of Greek builders – opened up the possibility of reacting to the topical challenge of new iron construction.

To traditional architecture, iron presented a real threat to the tectonic mode of expression because its load-bearing dimensions seemed too weak. Unlike Bötticher, however, Semper never speculated on the possibility of finding an expression for iron construction that would be as equally satisfying as that which classical and Gothic architecture had found for stone. He reacted to the threat posed by iron in that he made the issue of destruction of matter more extreme (a 'carnival candle's glow') and declared it to be the most important principle in architecture. Matter should (like marble for the Greeks) be masked, yet not lead to any arbitrary form of decoration. For the design of surfaces, Semper postulated two important conditions: firstly, the mask must sit on the material ('masking does not help where what is behind the mask is wrong');[4] secondly, he associated the design of the mask with the Greek word *kosmos,* which, aside from world order, means ornament, as expressed in the word 'cosmetic'. This double meaning of cosmos and cosmetic was what Semper hoped to achieve in the mask-like appearance of a building. The epidermis thus becomes the site of a dialogue between building issues and world orders or, better, between concealed presence and represented outside world. Added to this, the matter behind the mask lends the cosm(et)ic dimension of stability and permanence.

Monolithic Holes

In the early 1960s, Donald Judd introduced high-tech materials such as aluminium and Plexiglass into art. He called them 'specific', since materiality and surface finish here predicate each other and cannot be separated materially. One could surmise that the 'specific objects', as Judd himself designated his three-dimensional works and to which he devoted a programmatic text of the same title in 1965,[5] are nothing other than a presentation of certain material characteristics. However, this is not the case.

Judd used the high-tech materials as a vehicle to arrive at a 'new architecture'[6] of objects that, although they exhibit the same characteristics as the high-tech materials, nonetheless embody these in a different aggregate condition – as three-dimensional objects and not merely as materials.

Even if the 'specific objects' belong to the genre of sculpture, they are phenomenologically closer to painted works. Judd, who was first a painter, observed that colour appears to be much more powerful when it is three-dimensionally formed (as in the case of a Harley-Davidson) than when it is merely applied to a flat surface (as in the case of traditional painting). What interested him was 'the thing as a whole; its quality as a whole', in which complexity is found in format and not in the internal ordering of parts. Thus 'the shape, image, colour and surface … are single and not particular nor scattered parts'. Colour becomes an object that, on the one hand, encloses space and, on the other, relates the enclosed space to the space around it. Despite their monolithic closedness, the 'specific objects' function as sounding vessels to open the enclosed space to the outside to the maximum.

This ambivalence is something completely different from the gradual differentiation of revealing/concealing or of presentation/representation. Here the issue is one of the simultaneous articulation of opposites: the viewer is confronted with a closed volume but nonetheless thinks the whole time only of the spatial relationships between enclosed and surrounding space. Robert Morris calls this the 'extroverted inclusiveness'

Herzog & de Meuron, Library of the Eberswalde Technical School, Eberswalde, Germany, 1994–99

This page
North elevation.

Opposite
Second-floor plan.

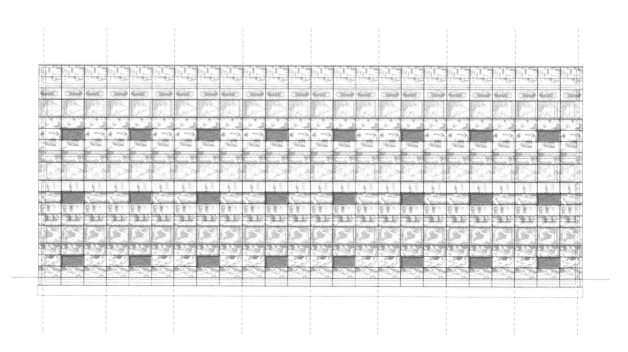

that characterises minimal art as opposed to the 'introverted exclusiveness' of classical modern art.[7] Picking up on this, it could also be said that the issue for 'specific objects' (as works of minimal art) is the true communication between an object and the context, while in the other case everything runs to a solipsistic monologue, a representation of an object in a context.

Monad Inside Out

In the past 10 years, architects Herzog & de Meuron have gained notice with their experiments with printed surfaces (the Ricola Building in Mulhouse, Cantonal Apothecary in Basel and Sport Center Pfaffenholz in St Louis). In the library of the Fachhochschule in Eberswalde, near Berlin, they took this type of surface treatment to limits never before attempted. Like an exotic alien the simple building volume, 'tattooed' over and over with images, juts out in its environment of conventional suburban row-houses. From Semper the cosmetic; from Judd the closed container form.

The library is fitted into three large, tub-shaped spaces surrounded by a sheath of concrete and glass panels. The motifs with which these panels have been imprinted were cut out of newspapers by the artist Thomas Ruff. Panels on the same layer have been printed with the same motif. In the vertical direction there are 17 panels showing a total of 13 different motifs: the motif on top depicts an enlarged cropping from the lowest one. One motif takes up two layers; one uses three layers (refugees during the building of the Berlin Wall, 1961). In addition, three motifs are especially prominent in that they are printed on glass and are higher by nearly half the size of the images on the concrete panels (110 x 150 centimetres rather than 75 x 150 centimetres).

The architectural reality behind these images points towards a certain iconographic intention of these motifs. On the other hand, the vertical sequences and horizontal series create a movement to the building volume that is not unlike a movie picture show. It is as if the library were a monad turned inside out, on the inner surfaces of which, now turned outside, is running a topical cultural state of affairs. No doubt the architects in this way pay tribute to the general conditions of mediaisation. And it is precisely to these images distributed by the media that they give matter – images that since Victor Hugo's *ceci tuera cela* have been suspected of sucking off the last bit of matter clinging to architectural surfaces.

In diametrical opposition, Herzog & de Meuron attempt to infuse new life into architectural reality through mediaisation. The images here do not represent an attack on architectural matter; much rather they generate a virtual movement of matter. In Semper's sense, the roots of the surface movement go back to the cosmetic and not to technical manipulation. The movement is that of a decidedly static matter.

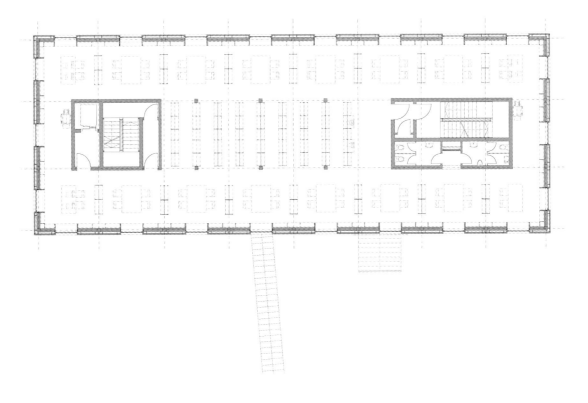

Herzog & de Meuron,
Kramlich Residence and
Media Collection, Oakville,
Napa Valley, California, us,
1997–2003

Below
First-floor plan.

Opposite top
Night view of the roof top.

Opposite bottom
Model study. Working with
more complex floor plans,
Herzog & de Meuron are
turning their use of
diagrammatic surfaces
inside as well as out. The
em-placement of an object
in the world is being
seamlessly related to the
the em-placement of a
world into an object.

Diagrammatic

Semper, Judd, and Herzog & de Meuron used
technical innovations (iron, high-tech materials,
and media) to transform the architectural surface
into something nonrepresentational. They shove a
bolt in the door of solipsistical self-presentation,
the game of revealing/concealing, in that they
cover the surfaces with hermetical layers of
colour and images. They make these surfaces the
site of an exchange between the architectural
work and the world outside – the cosmos in
Semper's case, the spatial context in Judd's, the
moving image of time in Herzog & de Meuron's.

In this context it is better to speak of an em-
placement in the sense of placing a building in a
context. The expression of em-placement begins
at the point where representation ceases. Being
open here connotes a factual openness in the face
of the other, the outside, and the stranger while
representation is merely self-exhibition to the outside
world. Therefore, the character of em-placement is
diagrammatic. It relates that which opposes the
figurative quality of an architectural work and impinges
upon it from the outside into the building's own design.
A diagrammatic surface represents nothing, conceals
nothing, reveals nothing. Rather it opens passages for
fleeing the prison of the architectural representation.

New Architecture?

Just as representation exists at the cost of outer
space (the space from which one observes), one
could also say that the diagrammatic exists at the
expense of inner space (a characterless interior of
a masked building). We then find in the whole history
of modern architecture the thematisation of the
surfaces compensated and crossed over by another
theme: the destruction of the box that leads to the
nullification of the border – the surface between

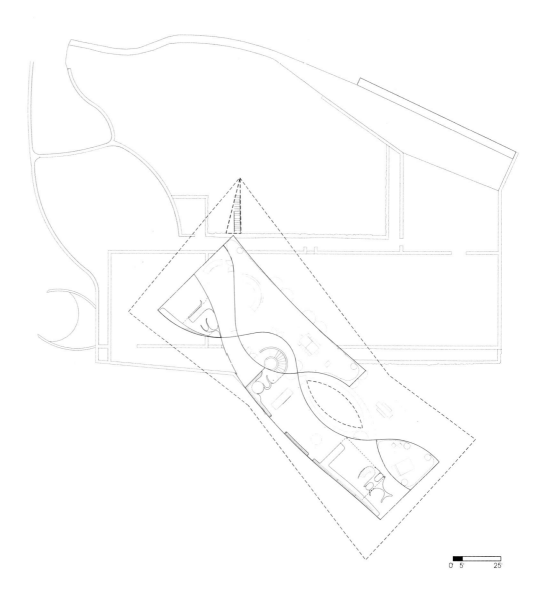

0' 5'   25'

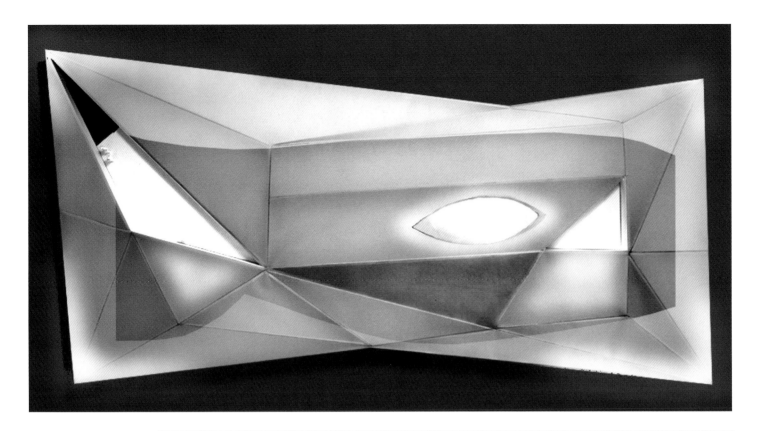

Notes
1. See for example Terence
Riley, *Light Construction*,
The Museum of Modern Art
(New York), 1995.
2. Gottfried Semper,
*Der Stil in den technischen
und tektonischen Künsten
oder praktische Aesthetik:
Ein Handbuch für Techniker,
Künstler und Kunstfreunde*,
vol 1, Verlage für Kunst und
Wissenschaft (Frankfurt),
1860, p 231.
3. Carl Bötticher, *Die Tektonik
der Griechen*, 2 vols, F. Riegel
(Potsdam), 1842–52.
4. Semper, op cit, p 232.
5. Donald Judd, 'Specific
Objects', *Arts Yearbook*, 1965;
also Donald Judd, *Complete
Writings, 1959–75*, New York
University Press (Halifax/New
York), 1975.
6. Robert Smithson, 'Donald
Judd', in *7 Sculptors*, Institute
of Contemporary Art
(Philadelphia), 1965;
also Nancy Holt (ed)
*The Writings of Robert
Smithson*, New York University
Press (New York), 1979.
7. Robert Morris, 'Notes
on Sculpture. Part 3: Notes
and Non Sequiturs', *Artforum*,
vol 5, no10, Summer 1967,
pp 24–29.

inside and outside – to thus make possible one continuous flow of space.

Until recently it would have seemed quite obvious to designate Herzog & de Meuron as specialists in the surface and the vertical, thus differentiating them from other architects who work in the first place with horizontal plans (such as Rem Koolhaas). But lately there have been signs that Herzog & de Meuron are also working with more complex floor plans. This can be explained less as the inappropriate takeover of other colleagues' strategies than as the logical consequence of the diagrammatic surface itself, since the diagrammatic can just as well be turned inside as outside.

The em-placement of an architectural object in the world at large can be turned around, in that a world can be em-placed in an object (like a monad) or both can be harnessed together, in that the em-placement of an object in the world is seamlessly related to the em-placement of a world into an object. Thus seen, the Kramlich Residence can be understood as the first realisation of a coherent passage between a vertical and a horizontal order, between dividing surfaces and flowing space, between matter and the destruction of matter. It can here be seen how the outer world breaks into the inner, and also how the real world can be layered over with the virtual. In the latter, the cosmetic plays just as important a role for the creation of spaces as does transparency. The position of the entwined transparent surfaces generates a labyrinthine fabric of partitions while their cosmetic treatment installs spatial cores inside the labyrinth. As opposed to representative surfaces, diagrammatic surfaces do not reconnect on a representational level what they separate, but interpret and interpolate spatial differences between the two sides. ∆

Translated from the German by Claire Bonney.

From Microcosm to Macrocosm:

The Surface of Fuller and Sadao's US Pavilion at Montreal Expo '67

For Buckminster Fuller, the surface was never just simply cladding or expression of materials, but rather the representation of ideas in an active and engaged manner. Though the skin of his United States Pavilion for the Montreal Expo '67 was likened to that of an orange or animal skin, Fuller was in fact interested in how a surface could mimic the sensitivity of the human skin – letting in light and porosity – allowing it to operate as an animated smart surface. **Timothy M Rohan** describes how the origins of the surface of the geodesic Expo sphere derived from Fuller's thinking about cartography and politics, which can be traced back to his Dymaxion Map projects of the 1930s and 1940s.

Modernist dreams came true at Montreal Expo '67. The modules of Moshe Safdie's Habitat were heralded by admirers as a workable prototype for the mass production of housing, while the acrobatic plastic forms of Frei Otto's West German Pavilion were extolled as the culmination of experiments with catenary roofs that went back to the late 1930s. Other pavilions, like the vast pyramidal Gyotron amusement centre, energetically worked through the repertoire of structural forms, such as the space frame and the megastructure, that had been in development since the Second World War. A writer for one architectural journal exulted: 'Montreal Expo '67 is a brilliantly ordered visual world – and almost everyone loves it'.[1]

In contrast to these earthbound forms, Buckminster Fuller's lightweight, spherical United States Pavilion rose above the fairgrounds like some strange new planet. It too was a brilliant structural exercise, but it featured an equally provocative surface composed of thousands of acrylic plastic minidomes that were clear but mysteriously clouded by clusters of sun shades, giving it a slightly uncanny quality. Renowned critic Umberto Eco, in his review of the Expo, said that he preferred the pavilion to all the others because it had an 'intangible' and 'ambiguous' character different from the familiar narrative told by its exhibitions within.[2]

Though it would be anachronistic to read our contemporary preoccupation with the surface into Fuller's work, the experimental exterior of this sphere is so rich in mechanical ingenuity and metaphor that it can aid us in exploring Fuller's overall system of thought. For Fuller, the surface is never simply a cladding or expression of materials, as in most architecture. It is instead a field for the representation of ideas in an active and engaged manner. Indeed, the origins of the surface of the Expo sphere derive from a line of development in Fuller's thinking about cartography, politics and skin that can be traced from his Dymaxion Map projects to his concept of the World Game, which was his initial proposal for Expo '67. This brief account of the Expo pavilion will look in particular at how long before late-20th-century architectural discourse focused upon these subjects Fuller used the metaphors of map and skin to explore the potential of the surface for the future of the geodesic dome.

During the 1950s and 1960s, Fuller had designed a string of geodesic domes for exhibition purposes, but the United States Pavilion was the most impressive of them all. Using geodesic geometry, Fuller and his associate, architect Shoji Sadao, designed a three-quarters transparent sphere that embodied the universality of a world's fair. The pellucid transparency

of the plastic surface made the contents visible from the outside – a sign of the openness of American society meant to contrast with the hermetic forms of the nearby Soviet Pavilion. Inside, the exhibitions were conceived around the theme of 'Creative America' and featured sections on Pop Art, Hollywood and the space programme that were arranged on an independent series of platforms designed by Cambridge Seven Architects.

What made the Expo sphere different from Fuller's earlier domes or the other pavilions was its experimental surface. At first glance it seemed similar to his other experiments with double-shell domes, but it was a far more heterogeneous mesh of structure and surface than anything his design team had attempted before. For the Montreal Expo, Fuller and Sadao took a space frame and warped it into a sphere with an open outer layer of triangular octet units of welded-steel pipe and an inner layer of hexagonal frames held together by a webbing and sealed from the outside by thousands of acrylic plastic minidomes. The contrasting geometries of the frameworks and the additional layer of projecting minidomes imbued the surface with an admirably clear yet complex optical quality. Indeed, this 'lacy filigree' – as several critics called it – was so complex that it is difficult to say where structure ended and surface began.

In addition to being a technological feat, the surface can be understood as a representation of Fuller's cosmology. The basic unit of the surface,

the minidome, of course referred to one of the primary forms of Fuller's geometric system: the dome. The surface was therefore self-referential to the non-Cartesian systems of geometry that he had been working on for more than four decades. At the same time, this sphere that was itself composed of domes was the visual embodiment of Fuller's idea of the 'macro-micro-oscillocosm' or 'the microcosm within the macrocosm'. This phrase lay at the basis of Fuller's concept of an ideal and nonhierarchical world order confirmed by the existing order found in nature. Broadly speaking, he believed that nature beginning with minute elements like the molecule, the atom or the cell and building up into larger structures, was an equitable, self-regulating and ideal system that human beings should look to as a model for their political and economic institutions.[3]

This political idealism played a role in Fuller's original designs for Expo '67 and informed his concept of surface as well. When first asked to provide a design for the US Pavilion in 1964, Fuller had suggested that it could become a venue for his visionary concept of the World Game. This would have been a giant electronic version of his flexible Dymaxion Map, coded with information about resources and current events fed by computers from around the world that visitors could manipulate, almost like a video or computer game, to make the best decisions about US domestic and foreign policy. Rather than seeing exhibitions about the artistic, commercial and political activities of the US, visitors would have been invited to make policy decisions using this animated surface. Fuller later claimed that even in 1964 he knew that the quagmire of the Vietnam War would send the international reputation of the US to its

lowest ebb by the time the Expo got under way, and that his World Game would be a tool to correct the situation.[4]

Political idealism informs Fuller's surfaces. Without going into too much detail, it is important to know that the Dymaxion Map upon which the World Game was based, itself played a key and recurring role in Fuller's unique surface-consciousness. It had first been conceived by Fuller in the late 1930s as a flexible world map made up of 14 manipulable triangular and square facets that more accurately depicted the surface of the earth than the traditional but distorted Mercator projection cantered upon the Atlantic. These facets could also fold up into a polyhedral globe, thus overcoming the discrepancies between flat map and three-dimensional globe that had long confounded cartographers.

Fuller published the map in *Life* magazine in 1943 so that readers could cut out and manipulate the facets for themselves to get a sense of the shifting and ever-changing perspectives of the various powers that had led to the world war. He compared the exercise to peeling and flattening the 'skin of an orange'. Fuller said that he was putting into action a 'fluid geography' that could help make ordinary citizens into 'political geographers'. This analysis of the surface of the earth using great circle geometry has been credited with ultimately leading to Fuller's invention of the geodesic dome.[5] It is noteworthy that the origins of Fuller's thinking about surface and structure lie in cartography – a flat graphic means of analysis

that at this time was rarely considered in conventional architectural discourse – rather than construction, as is the case for most architects.

In his initial World Game scheme for Expo '67, Fuller intended to dramatically re-encapsulate his own development of this 'mutable map' in a kind of spectacular floor-show of Dymaxion gymnastics. Visitors to the pavilion would have first seen a 250-foot diameter globe that would mechanically transform into a polyhedron and then relax, like an 'animal skin' or bearskin rug, into a flat Dymaxion map like a board game upon which the World Game could be played out. Fuller was fascinated with structures and surfaces that could fold and collapse. This 'pre-Deleuzian' folding action can even be interpreted as an attempt to express his idea of 'fluid geography'.[6] Most importantly, what emerges here is that for Fuller the surface is active, game-like and information rich.

After Fuller's client, the United States Information Agency, rejected the World Game as unfeasible, the project underwent a metaphorical shift. Fuller reconceived the pavilion as a geodesic three-quarter sphere with a diameter of 76 metres and a height of 61 metres. Working with Sadao, he envisioned it as a 'giant valve' that would be the ultimate 'controlled environment' with a transparent and flexible skin. 'From the inside there will be uninterrupted visual contact with the exterior world,' Fuller said. 'The sun and the moon will shine in, the landscape and sky will be completely visible, but the unpleasant effects of climate, heat, dust, bugs, glare, etc. will be modulated by the skin to provide a "Garden of Eden" interior.'[7] Other domes, like the St Louis Climatron of 1960 – a botanical garden Fuller also called the 'Garden of

architectural design

July 1967   Price 5s.

MONTREAL

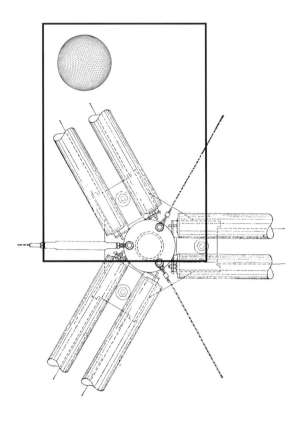

Eden' – were intended to be actual microcosms of the earth's environment.

The surface of the Montreal sphere also attests to Fuller's investigation of nature at its most microscopic level. He had long been interested in biological forms as representations of the 'microcosm in the macrocosm'. Indeed, the faceted spherical shape of the Expo sphere resembled a radiolarian – one of the marine microorganisms described in D'Arcy Thompson's *On Growth and Form* that had intrigued Fuller since the early 1950s.[8] Other biological metaphors fascinated him as well. In both the Dymaxion Map and the World Game projects he had referred to the surface as an orange or animal skin. Of course to talk about the surface of a building as a skin was common in tall building design, especially with the advent of the glass curtain wall, and skin has also become an inspiration for recent design activity.[9] Fuller explored this notion of skin more literally by turning to the cells of the human skin to validate his ideas about the surface of the Expo pavilion; 250 of the domes at the top of the sphere would release hot air and humidity through a valve that would function like a giant pore. He later said that it was this aspect of the project that had the most potential for the geodesic dome.

Fuller mused:

Anyone looking at the geodesic dome in Montreal saw a very beautiful piece of mechanics … It is possible, as our own human skin, all of our pores, all of the cells organize, so that some are photo-sensitive and some are sound-sensitive, and they're heat sensitive, as it would be perfectly possible to create a geodesic of a very high frequency where each of these pores could be circular tangencies of the same size. One could be a screen, others breathing air, others letting light in, and the whole thing could articulate just as sensitively as a human being's skin. And I really think geodesic domes such as that will be developed.[10]

Something of the folding action of the World Game project would also be retained in the Expo sphere in Fuller's attempts to devise a flexible system of shades to shield the interior from the sun. He believed that it was this aspect that anticipated the development of a photosensitive surface. Over a hundred years before, Joseph Paxton had devised an ingenious but labour-intensive system of Venetian blind-like shades for his Crystal Palace. In contrast, Fuller's shades would be mechanised and intelligent in that they were controlled by computer. He intended that six times during the course of the day, 4700 aluminised triangular shades rolled up within the tubes of the inner hexagonal framework would

Above and hereafter
The July 1967 'Montreal' issue of *Architectural Design* was devoted to the 1967 World Exhibition. Five pages were exclusively given over to Buckminster Fuller's US Pavilion.

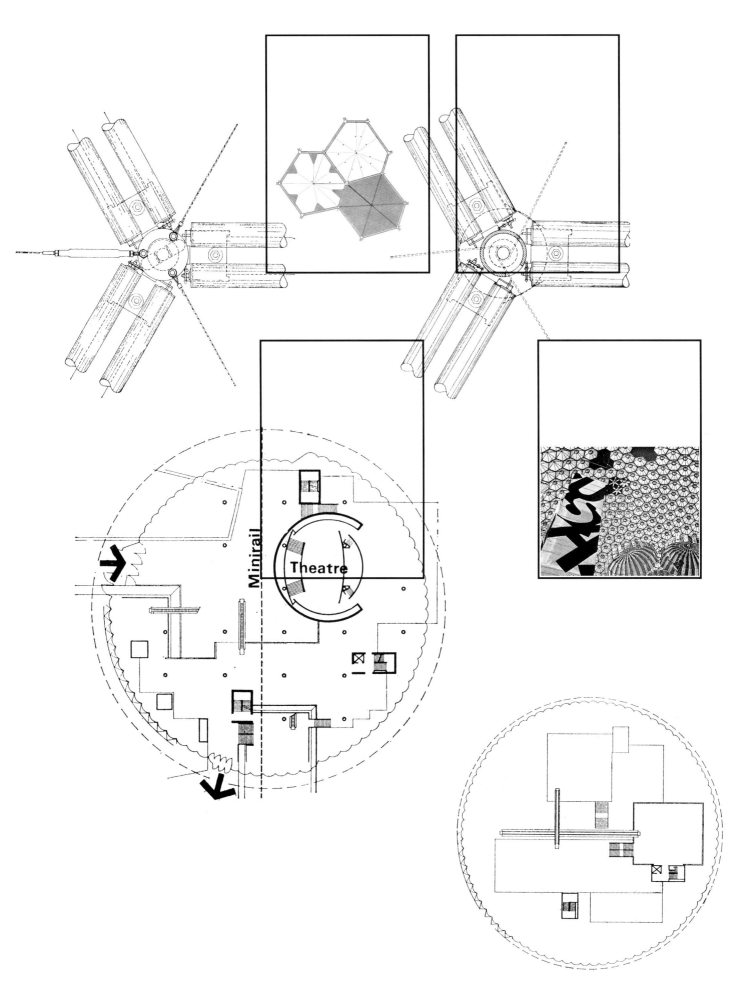

Minirail

Theatre

Notes
1. Mildred Schmertz, 'Brilliantly ordered visual world', Architectural Record, vol 142, July 1967, p 115.
2. Umberto Eco, 'A theory of expositions', Dot Zero, no 4, Summer 1967, p 9.
3. Author's conversation with Shoji Sadao, 6 August 2002. See also Robert W Marks, The Dymaxion World of Buckminster Fuller, Reinhold (New York), 1960, pp 7–13.
4. R Buckminster Fuller, 'World Game, how it came about', 50 Years of the Design Science Revolution, Carbondale, World Resources Inventory/Southern Illinois University (Illinois), 1969, pp 111–18.
5. Thomas W Leslie, 'Energetic geometries: the Dymaxion Map and the skin-structure fusion of Buckminster Fuller's geodesics', Arq, vol 5, no 2, 2001, pp 161–70.
6. Mark Wigley, 'Planetary homeboy', Any, no 17, pp 16–23. For more on the fluidity between plane and sphere, see p 21. This article is about the Geoscope projects of the 1950s that form an important intermediary stage between the Dymaxion Map and the World Game.
7. Fuller, quoted in 'Bucky's biggest bubble,' Architectural Forum, June 1966, vol 124, pp 74–79.
8. Joachim Krausse and Claude Lichtenstein (eds) Your Private Sky: R Buckminster Fuller, the Art of Design Science, Lars Müller Publishers & Museum für Gestaltung Zurich (Baden), 1999, pp 442–44.
9. Ellen Lupton's exhibition 'Skin: Surface, Substance and Design', 7 May–15 September 2002, and the catalogue of the same name for the Cooper-Hewitt Museum, New York, explore the potential of skin as an inspiration for design. See especially Alicia Imperiale, 'Digital skins: The architecture of surface,' in Ellen Lupton (ed) Skin: Surface, Substance and Design, Princeton Architectural Press (New York), 2002.
10. R Buckminster Fuller, 'Geodesic domes: A human being's skin', Domebook 2, 1971, p 91.
11. Ibid, p 91.

unfurl in different patterns following the course of the sun to shade the interior. The shades, grouped in units of 18 (three hexagons of six shades each), would be controlled by miniature motors that received information from a central 'punch tape' computer – making this a smart surface though one not nearly as informed and articulate as that which Fuller had contemplated for the World Game. Fuller hoped that when entire sections of the aluminised shades blossomed and shone at times in accordance with the movements of the sun, the surface would be animated with a fascinating moving quality.

As with so many of Fuller's projects, this was a good idea but one that was not feasible at the time. Though the shades worked in the studio where a prototype functioned under ideal conditions, an inadequate lubricating agent caused the motors to freeze up soon after the pavilion was completed. The shades remained permanently open in various configurations. Even so, the outline of these mysterious blotch-like forms upon the surface of the sphere still offered some shade and proved to be visually compelling. Though Fuller is not usually credited with having much of an interest in or sense of aesthetics, the pavilion was widely considered 'beautiful'. Fuller himself said: 'It did all kinds of things to your intuition'.[11]

Striking and well received though the Expo pavilion was, it would have a greater impact upon the world of science than of architecture. Two young scientists, Harold Kroto and Richard Smalley, who attended the Expo, would be inspired by the complexity of the sphere to search for a new class of carbon molecules, which many years later in 1985 they would name the 'Fullerine' and win a Nobel Prize for along with Robert Curl. In fact, the Expo skin is perhaps of greater importance as a model of Fuller's idealism and a source of inspiration for thinking about the surface in a more active, information-rich or biological manner than as an actual model. Unfortunately, even seeing the skin of the Expo sphere is now impossible since in 1975 the plastic minidomes were destroyed in a disastrous fire and now only a ghostly skeleton remains. ∆

The author would like to thank Shoji Sadao, Edward Baum and Neil Levine.

In Search of the
Plasma Membrane

For **Michael Trudgeon**, boundaries offer the possibilities of being blurred and porous, opaque rather than sharply delineated and transparent. His project for a screen lounge in a Melbourne museum draws on the vocabulary of video and film production while simultaneously taking its architectural inspiration from the latticework and screens of 16th-century Mogul India. An attempt to build the thin translucent surface favoured by digital rendering, the thin-skin plasma membrane is realised as a discontinuous and fragmented surface comprised of several layers.

The footprints in the sand, the thin furrow drawn with the stick, are already steps toward the continuous representation of the boundary. When the wind erases them, when the rain washes them away, the step is taken to a permanent demarcation through a row of field stones, a hedge, or a fence.[1]

The act of design or architectural intervention is the drawing of a line in the sand. Territories are created by such gestures on either side of that line. Their significance may be perceptual, proprietorial, social or organisational, demarcating significant differences. How that line is understood, elaborated on, processed, expanded and celebrated becomes part of the momentum of the social context or event space that also creates the impetus for such actions and sustains them.

For Raymond Loewy and the 'skin doctors' of early American industrial design, the boundary or surface was an expression of efficiency and optimism. It presented a slippery simplicity, obfuscating the complex internal uncertainties of the mechanical within. This opaqueness stands in strong contrast to the contemporary trend to expose and dramatise these processes through the use of transparent and translucent skins. While adding nothing to the user's understanding of the machine, this dramatisation can be engaging and diverting.

The notion of the surface as a fixed skin, a stable and opaque signifier by which the viewer recognises and knows the entity or object, has given us the model of the classical body. Communication technology, medical-imaging techniques, remote sensing and computer-enhanced visualisations give us the extended body, the body as data set, the enhanced body, the virtual body, the immersed body and the lost body. This transformation and augmentation in identifying and specifying objects, buildings and spaces has fuelled the pursuit of process-driven indeterminate boundaries and surfaces.

For the architect Cedric Price, the idea of a building is pursued and understood as a system of environmental control rather than as an enclosure or legible envelope. The building or boundary is seen as performative, designed to catalyse and accommodate change.[2] The meaning or content of the space is expressed through transaction, the process of information exchange. Here the building is significant as a generator or filter. The surfaces are not passive markers but dynamic fields that mediate or stimulate the flow of information, inviting experience.

Jeremy Rifkin, in *The Age of Access*, identifies the rise of the experience economy and a world informed by contingency and indeterminacy, a world not of truths but scenarios and options. Within this protean reality the world is full of responsive, shape-shifting identities and personae, an entirely performative perspective.[3]

Computer-rendering packages have allowed designers and architects to celebrate this desire for an indeterminate, diaphanous shimmering skin, offering, like the dance of the seven veils, a glimpse of something unimaginably exquisite, something forever shifting and changing; an enfolding plasma membrane.

The idea of the blurred and porous boundary, somehow responsive, eliciting intrigue while at the same time being inexpensive and easy to detail, has been preoccupying me. For a recent Melbourne commission we have been developing nomadic and reconfigurable semi-private media-viewing pods for use in a public museum space dedicated to exhibitions of the moving image. These screen lounge pods have been

Michael Trudgeon and David Poulton (computer visualisation Glynis Teo)

Previous page
Detail of louvred surface showing mesh membrane lounge pod. Seeing through to the inner padded wall and the view beyond, through the perforations, all reflected in the outer skin of the mirror-coated louvres and assembled to create a discontinuous porous surface.

Above
Exploded view of layered skin of screen lounge pod and semi-private media-viewing pavilion. The composite surface of a perforated inner padded wall, mesh core and outer layer of louvres can be seen on the right.

designed for use by small groups of people to view video on demand, play computer games, surf the Net and produce their own content for viewing by others within the museum. The pods have been designed to seat between two and six people.

We were keen to emphasise the idea of the flow of data and energy through the building spaces, to create spaces that were not readily determined immediately, with the intention of creating curiosity, with surfaces that wrapped around the lounge spaces but did not isolate them. Drawing from the vocabulary of video and film production we wanted to design an exterior skin that reflected this character, alluding to scanning, sampling and the jump cut, to create a discontinuous and fragmented porous surface that suggested the voyeuristic and participatory nature of television. We also saw this discontinuous nature as being reminiscent of the experience of the city.

The pods have been designed with an external skin of matt-finished reflective raw-aluminium panels and translucent fibreglass. This way the architectural forms and surfaces of the surrounding building are picked up and reflected in the surface of the pods. The 6-millimetre external skin is expressed at either end, projecting beyond the structural frame and emphasising its presence as a thin surface enfolding the space. The key presence of the pods is in fact their interiors, each monochromatically toned in one of the three colours of television: red, green or blue. These colours will be softly bounced off the reflective surfaces and beamed out into the surrounding gallery space.

The walls of the screen lounge pods consist of three layers. The outer surface of the pod is louvred to break down the solidity of the surface. Behind the louvres is a black mesh wall, the middle membrane. The louvres offer the illusion that the interior can readily be glimpsed, an invitation to voyeurism. In fact behind the

Above
Michael Trudgeon and David Poulton (computer visualisation Glynis Teo). Interior of screen lounge pod showing the inner padded skin perforated by an array of cluttered peepholes or viewing ports.

Right top
Marble screens at Jami Masjid Champanir, Gujerat, India, 1500–08 AD.

Right bottom
Detail of white marble screen with pierced geometric tracery at the tomb of Salim Chisti, Fatehpur Sikri, India, 1571 AD.

59

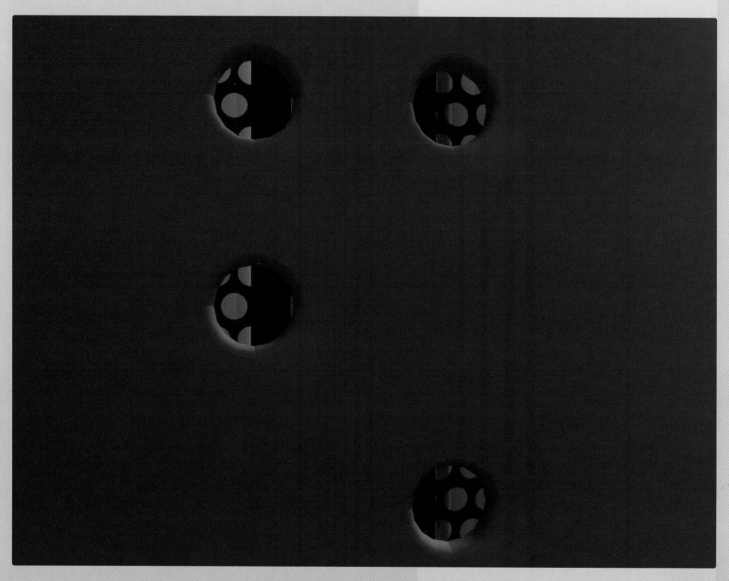

Michael Trudgeon and David Poulton (computer visualisation Glynis Teo)

Above
Middle mesh membrane of lounge pod seen from the interior through the perforation clusters in the inner padded wall.

Right
Full-scale maquette of the screen lounge pod showing the inner padded surface with perforation clusters.

Notes
1. August Schmarsow, *Das Wesn der Architektonischen Schöpfung*, Leipzig, 1894, p 5.
2. Mary Lou Lobsinger, 'Cedric Price: An architecture of the performance', *Daidalos* 74, 2000, pp 22–29.
3. Jeremy Rifkin, *The Age of Access*, Penguin (London), 2000.
4. Sophia and Stefan Behling, *Sol Power: The Evolution of Solar Architecture*, Prestel-Verlag (Munich), 1996, pp 116–19.

louvres and the mesh is a mostly solid wall with only a small number of peepholes that offer selected views into the interior. The inner surface of the louvres is mirrored so as to reflect and distort any image that does present itself from the interior. This achieves an amplification of the sense of activity from within while further fragmenting it. The passer-by, in motion, glimpses the peepholes discontinuously, in a row interrupted by the screening rhythm of the outer vertical louvres. This apparatus acts like a zoetrope, the early hand-held mechanical forerunner to cinema, creating a strange, slightly suspended sequence of fragmentary images. This is caused by the phenomenon of persistence of vision.

Viewed from the interior of the pod, the inner wall is padded, with an array of peepholes at eye level. From within, the occupant looks out through the padded wall and the black metal mesh beyond and out past the mirrored louvres to the surrounding space – the view of the outside now distorted and fragmented by the louvres.

Architecturally, the exterior marble lattices of the Mogul architects of the 16th century in northern India[4] and the shuttered, latticed, slatted, screened and fretworked envelopes of the lightweight timber houses of tropical Queensland, have provided us with the model of the indeterminate and porous skin. It is, however, the promise of the shimmering filmy plasma membrane that we dream of. ∆

Conveying 3-D Shape and Depth with Textured and Transparent Surfaces

Scientists and architects alike want to be able to look within structures while maintaining a view of the exterior skin or surface. **Victoria Interrante** explores the potential of transparent surface rendering as posed by scientific visualisation techniques. Here, she explores the very real problem of the dissolution of figure-ground relationships and the inevitable spatial oscillations that occur with digital transparency. She reviews the issues centred around rendering, while also presenting some novel graphic techniques that simultaneously enhance the representation of external surfaces and the visibility of internal structures.

In scientific visualisation there are many applications in which researchers need to achieve an integrated understanding of the three-dimensional shapes and relative depth distances of multiple overlapping objects. Transparent surface rendering has the potential to be a useful device in many of these cases for simultaneously portraying multiple superimposed structures in a single image, so that their complex spatial relationships can be more accurately and comprehensively inferred. The challenge is to determine how to portray the outermost objects in such a way that they can be both effectively seen and at the same time seen through

This article briefly reviews a variety of issues in transparent surface rendering and describes some novel graphical techniques that aim to enhance the representation of external transparent surfaces while maintaining the visibility of internal structures through the careful design and application of sparsely distributed opaque surface markings. Integral to this discussion is an analysis of the effects that various texture-pattern characteristics, such as orientation, have on surface-shape perception.

Notes
1. Andrew Blake and Heinrich Bülthoff, 'Shape from specularities: Computation and psychophysics', *Philosophical Transactions of the Royal Society of London*, B, 331, 1991, pp 237–52.
2. Donald D Hoffman and Whitman A Richards, 'Parts of recognition', *Cognition*, 18, 1984, pp 65–96.
3. Victoria Interrante, Henry Fuchs and Stephen Pizer, 'Enhancing transparent skin surfaces with ridge and valley lines', Proceeding, *IEEE Visualization* '95, 1995, pp 52–59.
4. Victoria Interrante, Henry Fuchs and Stephen Pizer, 'Conveying the 3D shape of smoothly curving transparent surfaces via texture', *IEEE Transactions on Visualization and Computer Graphics*, 3 (2), April–June 1997, pp 98–117.
5. In our experience, employing unevenly distributed texture has been problematic; when some areas are left devoid of texture while others are uniformly covered, the empty areas tend to be perceived as holes.
6. Victoria Interrante and Sunghee Kim, 'Investigating the effect of texture orientation on the perception of 3D shape', *Human Vision and Electronic Imaging VI*, SPIE 4299, 2001, pp 330–39.
7. The first principal direction is defined as the direction in which the surface curves most strongly, at a point. The second principal direction is the orthogonal direction in the tangent plane. On an elliptical surface, this will be the direction in which the surface is most flat. On a hyperbolic (saddle-shaped)

Above left, top and bottom
Incident light is specularly reflected by smooth, shiny materials in a preferred direction determined by the angle of incidence with respect to the surface normal. Thus, on a curved surface the highlight due to a given light source will appear to lie in a different position on the surface when viewed from one eye than when viewed from the other. Instead of perceiving the highlight to be in two locations at once, our visual system forms a single unified percept of the highlight floating in space. Psychologists have shown that people can use the direction of the displacement of the highlight to disambiguate bumps from depressions.[1]

Above right, top
Additive transparency.

Above right, bottom
Subtractive transparency.

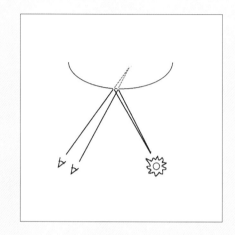

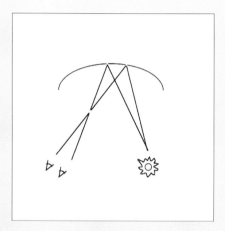

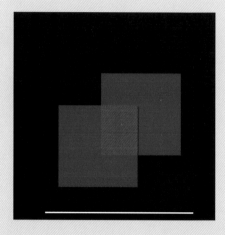

The Trouble with Plain Transparency

In computer-graphics images, as in everyday experience, smoothly finished external transparent surfaces can be surprisingly difficult to adequately perceive. The depth distance between an outer transparent surface and inner opaque entities can at times be so difficult to assess that even the depth-order relationships may appear ambiguous, and the subtle shading cues that might otherwise reveal the 3-D shape of a gently curving external transparent surface are often masked by the shading gradients of the underlying opaque inner structures.

Essentially the problem is a lack of sufficient information in the visual stimulus to allow an observer to accurately interpret either the geometry or the layout of the multiple objects in the scene. This complicates matters in that, in normal stereo vision, specular highlights are not perceived to lie on a reflective surface but rather appear to float in space either in front of the surface, if it is concave, or behind the surface if it is convex.[1]

Choosing an Appropriate Shading Model for Rendering a Transparent Surface

There are several common shading models that can be used to represent transparent surfaces. The choice of shading model is important because it affects the type of transparent surface that is simulated. One of the most commonly used models is additive transparency, in which the final intensity I at a point is defined as a linear combination, weighted by the surface opacity $\alpha \in (0,1)$, of the intensity I_f of the transparent surface and the intensity I_b of the background: $I = I_f a + I_b (1-\alpha)$. This model results in surfaces that appear to be made of gauze; when the surface is folded upon itself multiple times, the result converges to the colour of the transparent material. An alternative is subtractive or multiplicative transparency, in which the transparent surfaces are modelled as filters that impede the transmission of light, so that as multiple surfaces are overlapped the result gets progressively darker, tending towards black.

surface it will be the direction in which the surface curves most strongly in the opposite way.

8. Victoria Interrante, Sunghee Kim and Haleh Hagh-Shenas, 'Conveying 3D shape with texture: Recent advances and experimental findings', *Human Vision and Electronic Imaging VII*, SPIE 4662, 2002, pp 197–206.

9. Victoria Interrante, 'Illustrating surface shape in volume data via principal direction-driven 3D line integral convolution', *Computer Graphics, Annual Conference Series* (ACM SIGGRAPH 97), 1997, pp 109–16.

10. Detlev Stalling and Hans-Christian Hege, 'Fast and resolution independent line integral convolution', *SIGGRAPH 95 Conference Proceedings, Annual Conference Series*, 1995, pp 249–56.

11. Jack Goldfeather and Victoria Interrante, 'Understanding errors in approximating principal directions', ACM *Transactions on Graphics*, 2003, in press.

12. Wherever the order of the relative magnitudes of the first and second principal curvatures reverses, the first and second principal directions will switch places. At these points, which are referred to as 'umbilics', lines which are defined to follow the first principal direction will appear to rotate 90 degrees, creating a T-junction or corner in the flow field.

13. Sunghee Kim, Haleh Hagh-Shenas and Victoria Interrante,

Above left, top
A typical rendering of some of the multiple surfaces of interest in a radiation therapy treatment plan for prostate cancer.

Above left, bottom
An enhanced rendering in which opaque feature lines have been added along the major creases in the skin surface, with the intent to clarify the structure of the form and draw attention to the location of sensitive soft-tissue structures that have to be kept outside of any beam path.

Above right, top
A prototypical scientific data set involving layered transparent surfaces – a level surface of radiation dose enclosing an opaque treatment region.

Above right, bottom
An enhanced rendering of this data, in which the outer transparent surface has been augmented with a see-through texture designed to emphasise its shape.

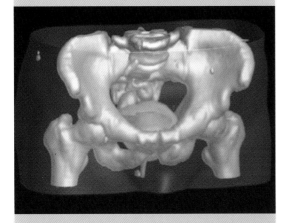

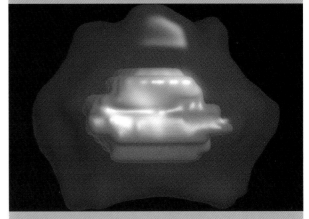

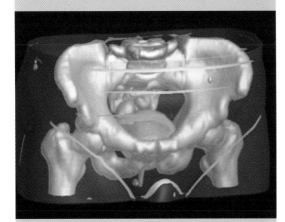

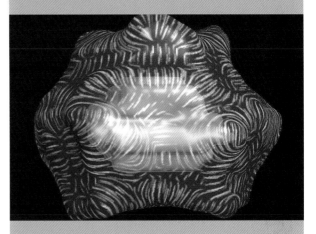

Emphasising Essential Lines

By adding detail in the form of sparse opaque markings to an external transparent surface, we have the potential to more effectively convey both its intrinsic shape features and its depth distance from underlying structures. The challenge is to decide what sort of markings will be most appropriate and to define an algorithm for determining how to place them over the surface. Silhouette lines are appropriate to enhance faceted objects, but on smoothly curving surfaces they can be problematic because they will not lie in the same place over the surface in the views from each eye. On complicated surfaces that exhibit multiple inflections of Gaussian curvature, valley lines can be useful for conveying important additional shape information. These lines are defined as the locus of points that lie at minima of negative curvature in the direction of greatest normal curvature over the surface, and their perceptual relevance is affirmed by research that suggests that people tend to subdivide objects into parts along their valley lines.[2] The pelvis renderings illustrate the use of valley lines on a transparent surface in a scientific visualisation application.[3]

Clarifying the Flow of the Form

Not all smoothly curving surfaces have shapes that can be well captured by a small set of feature lines. An alternative approach[4] is to apply a texture of uniformly distributed,[5] sparse opaque markings over the transparent surface. However, the choice of texture pattern, and how it is applied over the surface, has to be made with care. It is typically difficult to obtain suitable results using regular patterns such as stripes or spots, applied according to traditional solid or surface texture-mapping algorithms. What is needed is to create a pattern that is aesthetic, unobtrusive and of a style appropriate to the application, and to lay it over the surface in a way that emphasises rather than masks the curvature of the form.

A key question is: if one could design the perfect texture pattern to apply to any smooth surface in order to enable its shape to be more accurately and intuitively perceived, what would the essential characteristics of that texture pattern be? Recent research suggests that patterns with a strong directional component show shape best when the texture is everywhere oriented in the direction of maximum normal curvature[6] (the first principal direction);[7] textures that contain significant geodesic curvature, or turn in the surface, tend to mask surface shape,[8] whether the texture is defined by

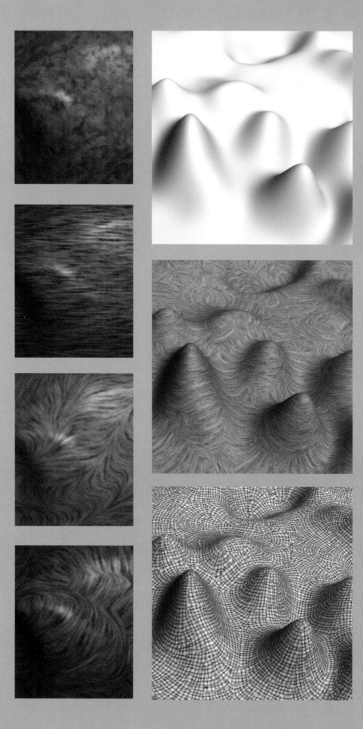

'Showing shape with texture –
two directions are better than
one', *Human Visions and
Electronic Imaging VIII*, 2003, in
press.
14. Gabriele Gorla, Victoria
Interrante and Guillermo
Sapiro, 'Texture synthesis for
3D shape representation', *IEEE
Transactions on Visualization
and Computer Graphics*, 2003,
in press.

Above left
Studies have found that how a
texture is oriented over a
surface can significantly affect
how accurately the surface
shape can be perceived –
anisotropic texture tends to
mask surface shape when the
direction of the anisotropy is not
aligned with the principal
directions of the form. From top
to bottom: An isotropic texture,
a uniformly oriented anisotropic
texture, an anisotropic texture
that turns in the surface, an
anisotropic texture that follows
the first principal direction at
every point.

Above right
Textures that follow both
principal directions appear to
show shape slightly more
effectively than textures that
follow only one. From top to
bottom: A smoothly shaded,
untextured surface, the same
surface textured with a line
integral convolution pattern
that follows the first principal
direction vector field at every
point, and the same surface,
textured with an orthogonal
grid pattern that is everywhere
aligned with both the first and
second principal directions.
© 1997 IEEE.

variations in surface colouration or by
variations in surface relief. Inspired by the
example of line drawings in medical
illustration, we have developed a volume-
rendering algorithm[9] in which 3-D line integral
convolution[10] is used to synthesise a solid
texture of sparse opaque strokes that
everywhere follow the vector field of first
principal directions over a transparent level
surface. With this method it is possible to
reliably portray a smoothly curving outer shell
of arbitrary shape in such a way that its 3-D
form and position in space can be adequately
understood in relation to the shapes and
locations of underlying interior structures.

The two primary technical challenges in
applying principal-direction texturing to
polygonal models are: to obtain accurate
estimates of the principal directions at every
vertex on the surface,[11] and to define a smooth and
consistently oriented first principal direction vector field
across the mesh. To finesse certain problems with the
latter,[12] it can be advantageous to use symmetric
textures that contain elongated components following
both principal directions rather than patterns that
follow the first principal direction only.[13]

Recently we have developed a new surface-texture
synthesis algorithm[14] that allows one to apply a broad
range of textures, including many photographically
acquired 2-D patterns, over arbitrary polygonal models
without seams or stretching, and in such a way that the
pattern is constrained to follow a predefined vector field
at a per-pixel level over the surface. We are actively
using this method to study shape-from-texture
perception, and are currently exploring ways in which it
can offer new promise for enhancing the representation
of 3-D shape in a wide variety of applications involving
textured and transparent surfaces. ◬

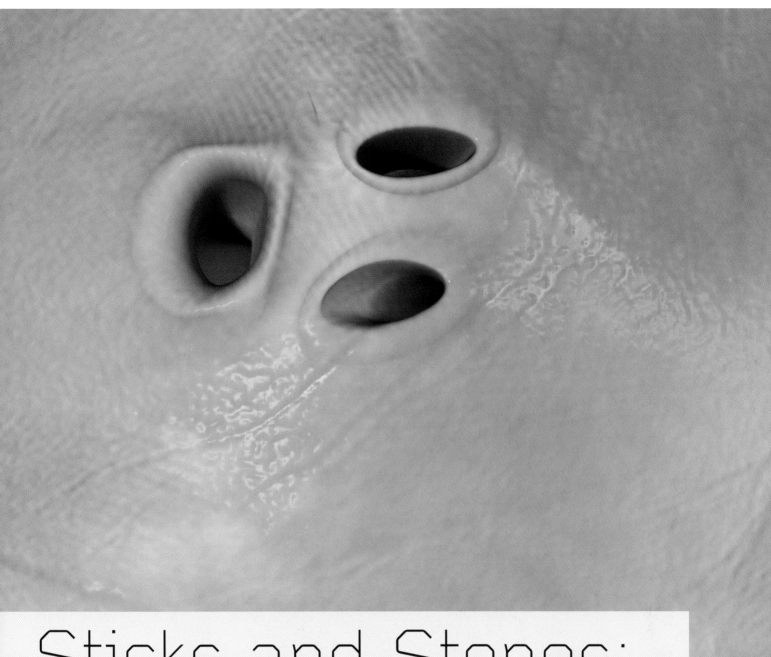

Sticks and Stones: Skins and Bones

Peter Wood differentiates between the dermis, which he denotes as a prime architectural state, and the digital surface that he regards as an artificial membrane. He likens the digital surface to the abandoned reptilian skin of a snake. Divorced from traditional moral codes relating to the body, it is architecturally 'immoral', cast off or removed from the bones of classicism and the fleshiness of modernism.

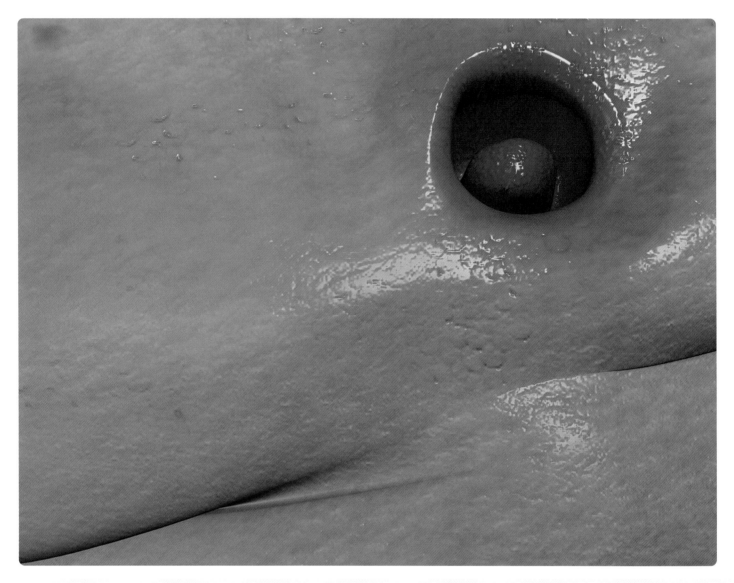

There is a riddle asked by children: 'What is the body's biggest organ?' Not the skeleton, lungs, brain or heart, but 'The Skin'. The human body's largest organ is the sack of dead and living cells that acts as our environmental envelope, protecting against the elements, against injury, against infection and (importantly) against every other organ escaping from that field we call 'The Body'. The trick of the riddle is this: skin is the invisible organ because it is visible, and its visibility is contingent on a categorical separation between seeing and touching.

Skin may be visible, but it 'sees' through its tactility. Skin is fundamentally different from our internal organs. The latter can be surgically removed leaving behind an intimate space, while the former is stripped from its support, which has the twofold effect of producing a flaccid simulacrum and a nude frame. The skin is not a surface but a primary architectural state. It encapsulates by defining a space that cannot otherwise be classed as complete. That it is discussed as a surface is symptomatic of our inability to accept that a plane can be measured with a volumetric quotient. Yet the skin is not simply a structure for the functioning of the body, it is also a fundamental sensory organ and it contributes to the delineation of a body in the phenomenological world. Skin is therefore a spatial filter between states, demarcating proprieties of interiority and exteriority – the traditional responsibility of architecture.

In architectural discourse, 'skin' is used to denote architectural surface. We might ask at this point why it is that so many digitally rendered architectural projects present architecture through skins of translucent and coloured gradations, devoid of location, dissolving in virtual domains. To be sure these apparitions are suited to a computer environment that allows images to float and layer, dissipate and liquefy, but what does that tell us about an architecture that has traditionally depended on stability, foundation and order? The digital skin appears separate and abandoned. These images have more in common with the skin of a reptile than that of a building: where the snake abandons a redundant translucent casing of its past surface, architecture increasingly seeks an opaque shell into which it can squeeze. Digital skins are not driven by traditional evolutionary factors and they reject what Alfonso Lingus describes as the 'carnal materiality' of skin:

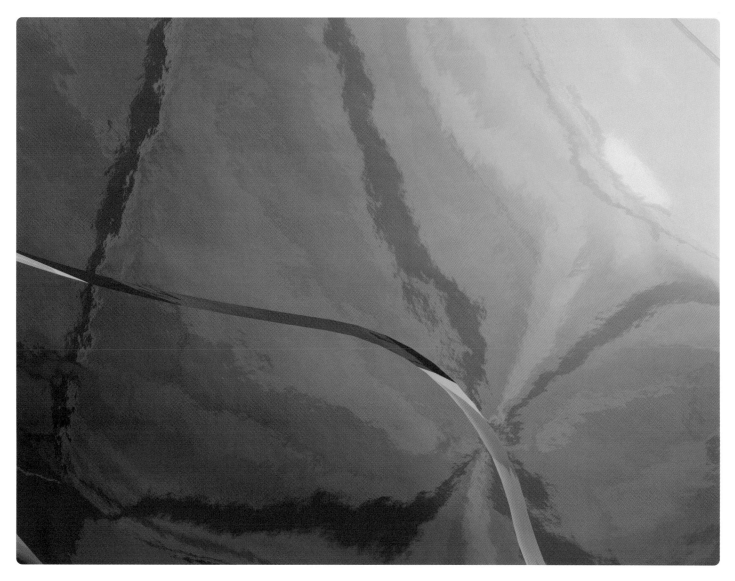

Skin is not hide nor covering, camouflage, uniform, adornment. It is a surface of exposure, zone of susceptibility, of vulnerability, of pain and abuse.[2]

The digital skin is wholly ornamental in so much as it has successfully separated itself from the body of canonical architecture. Since Semper, architecture has accepted that the white stones of antiquity are 'nakedness' brought about by the stripping away of an earlier polychromatic skin. It is this nudity that becomes the principal mask of Neoclassicism. Paradoxically the virtual skin represents a re-composition of a lost dermis of antiquity in the layers of coloured effect, but there is no longer a denuded body underneath. The virtual skin floats free of any metaphorical framework, and consequentially is divorced from traditional moral codes relating to the body. The virtual skin is immoral. It is removed from the bones of classicism, and the fleshiness of modernism. The virtual skin is cheap, disposable, replaceable – it is a new site of carnal materiality.

Jennifer Bloomer has observed that any desire architecture may have for virtual realities must reside in an attempt to repress the shame in its own body, the beauty of which is not even skin-deep.[3] That skin should have depth is exactly the problem under threat from virtual constructions of architecture. The membrane (weather envelope) that holds our bodies as complete and contained is stripped of its fat and fibre, and is held to the light as a hymen of translucent colour and texture. For Bloomer, fat occurs in the sexual organs; without fat we have no sexuality and therefore no reproductive capability. It hardly needs adding that it is fat that we crave when we discuss architectural taste.

Venturi, Brown and Izenour recognised this in Las Vegas with their physiognomy for a typical casino: 'The sign at the Dunes Hotel is more chaste: It is only two dimensional, and its back echoes its front, but it is an erection 22 stories high that pulsates at night'.[4] Theirs is an architecture of fat skins and bad taste (mess is lore) where the sign is a prophylactic architecture; a skin hung well over the bones of building, and the bigger the better. Relegating complexity and contradiction to postmodern romanticism, it follows that the latex prophylactic embraces complicity and contraception as its guiding mantra. The condom is emblematic of the architecture of late capitalism. It is a synthetic skin that rejects the biological model of skin as a cyclical system of renewal, and replaces it with a sterile artificial membrane.

Can it be a coincidence that the two most important architectural treatises of the last 25 years both place

Notes
1. Thomas Harris, *The Silence of the Lambs*, Arrow Books (London), 1999, p 196.
2. Alfonso Lingus, *Deathbound Subjectivity*, State University of New York Press (Albany, New York), 1989, p 138.
3. Jennifer Bloomer, '...and Venustas', *AA Files* 25, summer 1993, p 8.
4. Robert Venturi, Denise Scott Brown and Steven Izenour, *Learning from Las Vegas*, MIT Press (Cambridge, Mass, and London), 1972, p 53.
5. Robin Evans, *The Projective Cast*, MIT Press (Cambridge, Mass), 1995, p xxxi.
6. Joseph Rykwert, 'Greek temples: The polychromy', *Terrazzo* 2, Spring 1989, p 141.

Above
Patricia Piccinini, *Still Life with Stem Cells* 2002 (silicone, acrylic, human hair, mixed media, dimensions variable; Monash University Collection). Patricia Piccinini has been selected to represent Australia at the Venice Biennale 2003. This sculpture, which will 'live' in the Australian Pavilion during the festival, is of a realistic young girl caring for a group of strange embryonic lumps.

the condom on their covers. *Delirious New York* (at least in the more valuable first edition) utilises Madelon Vriesendorp's *Flagrant délit* to set a tone of architectural sterility where the Goodyear 'rubber' is cast aside post-coitus. For S,M,L,XL, Koolhaas cuts straight to the truth of phallic encasement where for architecture, like condoms, we like to believe that size counts. Architecture has been replaced by a disposable contraceptive skin that can be rolled seamlessly over an older world of questionable integrity. The digital skin is a simulacrum of sensory experience that displaces the tactility of the traditional skin with an artificial construction called 'texture'. The value of using a prophylactic is to inhibit the dangers implicit in the exchange of unstable elements despite the fact that exchange defines the act the condom attempts to limit – that of productive marking/making.

Architectural projection (it needs to be emphasised) is a mode of ejaculation: a sudden and fertile throwing. As Robin Evans has shown, for architecture to be truly productive it must insist on this projective casting, but the digital skin seeks to limit the points of transgression.

What connects thinking to imagination, imagination to drawing, drawing to building, and buildings to our eyes is projection in one guise or another, or processes that we have chosen to model on projection. All are zones of instability.[5]

We no longer seek to test the flesh beneath the surface of our architectural skins, as we no longer search for proof of a bodily association. We desire only that which we see, that which our eyes move across, and we avoid the points that facilitate volatile exchange – the places of touch, the places that smell ('Greek temples smelled. Obvious, is it not?').[6] The discipline of architecture is no longer interested in the invaginations of the skin. We have substituted the fold and crease for the guttural primacies of the gash and hole. Contingencies of closure (of the built or intellectual fabric of architecture) insist on the finality of completion. Architecture is less concerned with the skin per se than it is with where (and how) apertures in the hermetic skin can be sealed. The role of the architect has become one of camouflaging the points of closure. The moral responsibility of the architect has been reduced to providing the structural contingencies to protect against inappropriate disclosure – finding a place for the zip. ᗄ

Ornamental
Operations

A preoccupation with cultural concerns and ornament distinguishes the work of Melbourne-based architects Ashton Raggatt McDougall (ARM) from that of other experimental practices. In ARM's hands, digital tools are employed to produce an unruly ornamentality. Here **Brent Allpress** reviews ARM's unique approach as an operative abstraction in which cultural conventions of ornament give way to the cutting, marking and layering of shaped surfaces.

Significant shifts in the technical and economic constraints of industrial prefabrication are emerging through the development of digitally mediated drawing and manufacturing technologies such as CADCAM. Prefabricated components can potentially be mass-produced with variable or differentiated configurations without significant extra cost.

These technological developments have design implications that cannot be adequately accounted for solely in technical terms. Developing criteria for engaging with prefabricated differentiation is an emerging design problematic. Anachronistic cultural questions regarding the role and status of ornament also take on renewed relevance.

Standardised prefabrication was co-opted by modernist theory to promote cultural progress towards universal standards through a reductive logic of economic efficiency and technological progress. For Walter Gropius, standardisation provided a means to further develop Adolf Loos'

This page
The Kronberg Medical Clinic provides a digital prehistory to ARM's current practice. It was developed from a displaced photocopy of the iconic frontal photo of Robert Venturi's scheme for the Vanna Venturi House.

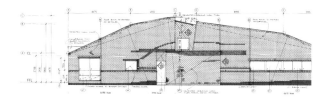

cultural and economic argument for progressing beyond ornament.[1] Gropius argued for standardisation based on universal formal principles. Bauhaus mass-production prototypes were to employ 'characteristic, primary forms and colours, readily accessible to everyone'.[2] This was to be an optimised and efficient modern architecture for the masses that was universally legible.

Modernism effaced aesthetic judgement through recourse to the external authority of a technical determinism. This tendency recurs in recent digitally designed architecture. The streamlined formal complexity of much of this work is not an inevitable outcome of technological progress. Architecture remains conditioned by nostalgia for the future.

Melbourne-based architects Ashton Raggatt McDougall (ARM) have established a diverse body of work employing digital representation and, more recently, computer-aided manufacturing. ARM's approach is differentiated from analogous international practice by the recurring cultural concerns that inform their projects and by their engagement with an unruly, digitally mediated ornamentality.

ARM's Kronberg Medical Clinic (1993) in Melbourne provides a digital prehistory to their current practice. This 'Not Vanna Venturi House' was developed from a displaced photocopy of the iconic frontal photograph of Venturi's scheme.[3]

This was pixilated to the scaled size of a brick module, providing a means to document an indistinct blurred condition. The project was then built in direct accordance with the image. Incidental artefacts captured by this mediating process were reinterpreted opportunistically as decorative brickwork relief.

The copy exceeded any servile postmodern referential relation to an original. The latent modernity of Venturi's work was solicited by exaggerating its asymmetry and horizontality. Frontal monumentality was forced into an engagement with a more marginal suburban orientation. The resulting misappropriated design takes on the rough surface qualities of a typical polychrome-brick suburban Melbourne building, challenging both source and site.

Howard Raggatt advocates the malapropic, a rhetorical device akin to catachresis, the trope of mis-use. ARM employs opportunistic misinterpretation and critical misuse of canonical precedent as a recurring design strategy. This is proposed as a characteristic cultural and contextual condition in the antipodes where the reception of international architectural culture is always already mediated. This scenario is ever more pervasive in the context of globalisation.

ARM's representational procedures are not a neutral mode of translation. Mediation enacts a motivated transfiguration. The curation of materialised output makes a decisive qualitative difference. This proto-digital process foreshadows ARM's subsequent engagement with CADCAM.

The recently completed National Museum of Australia (NMA) in Canberra, designed by ARM with

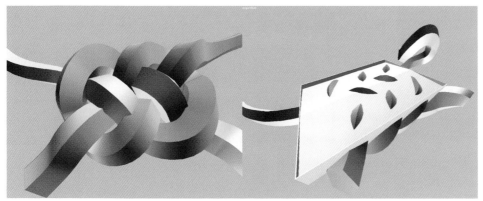

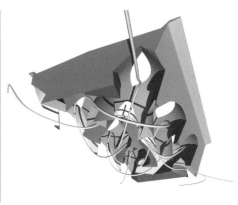

Ashton Raggatt McDougall, National Museum of Australia (NMA), Canberra, 2001

Opposite
At the NMA, ARM was called upon to produce a museum that both celebrates and critically reflects on the emerging identity and diversity of the nation. The interlocking building attempts to redeem the remnant aspirations of Walter Burley Griffin's partially implemented plan for the city. As can be seen here, ARM responded by producing buildings that form an unruly border to Acton Peninsula across the lake from the National Parliament.

Top, left to right
Boolean knot, Great Hall model and Boolean knot, and Boolean string intersecting the Great Hall, showing pentagonal Boolean subtraction. The axes of the NMA volumes are entangled within the Great Hall to create an extraordinary gathering space. This is the result of the Boolean subtraction of a gigantic computer-generated knot.

Left and above
Interior views of the Great Hall.

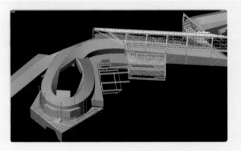

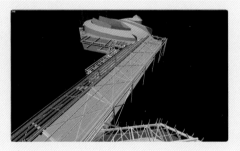

Ashton Raggatt McDougall,
National Museum of Australia
(NMA), Canberra, 2001

Above top
Aerial view.

Inset
Gallery of First Australians and
entrance canopy.

Above bottom (stretching to
opposite page)
Construction models of the
Gallery of First Australians.

Opposite
Exterior cladding of the Gallery
of First Australians.

Inset
Computer model of concrete-
cladding panel for the Gallery
of First Australians.

Robert Peck von Hartel Trethowan and Room 4.1.3 Landscape Architects, responds to a brief calling for a cultural museum that both celebrates and critically reflects on the emerging identity and diversity of the nation.[4]

Digital technologies play a generative role in the misappropriation of design precedent material and the transfiguration of surface materiality. Ornament is remotivated by a postcolonial cultural critique and employed to enact digitally mediated design operations, testing and exploiting the limits of legibility.

Walter Burley Griffin's partially implemented Canberra plan employed a grand geometry of landscape axes. ARM redeems the remnant aspirations of Griffin's plan by employing a landscape-scale ornamental interlace as a new axial urban figure. The interlocking NMA buildings form an unruly border to Acton Peninsula across the lake from the National Parliament. Sinuous computer-generated linear axial volumes have been extruded to trace out episodic meandering paths, void figures and framed views across the site. The axes are entangled within the interior of the Great Hall of the NMA to create an extraordinary gathering space that is the result of the Boolean subtraction of a gigantic computer-generated knot. For Raggatt, this subtractive negation forms a moulded void figure where ornament is 'nothing':

> Perhaps it is nothing if we mean something extra to the means of construction, something extra to the articulation of exposed structure, or something extra to the integrity of selected materials. Now instead of extras the primary volumes are subtractions but not in any kind of reductionist sense but rather literally, one figure subtracted from another. This is the idea of the volumes as cast, as the very origin of ornament, the reverse of ornament, rejected by ornament, yet it is also the means of production of ornament.[5]

The Great Hall windows that render the figure of the knot where it rends the surface of the building volume make oblique references to the Sydney Opera House fenestration redesigned by Australian architect Peter Hall after the competition-winning architect Jørn Utzon had quit the project. The precedent for a complex and difficult dialogue between local and international architectural culture was reaffirmed.

The Gallery of First Australians, devoted to indigenous Aboriginal culture, is housed within a black linear zigzag volume, infilled with literal built shadow lean-tos. The gallery is topped with a light-blue gable

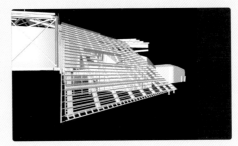

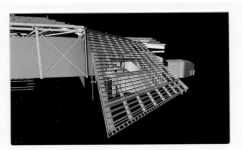

Notes

1. Walter Gropius, 'Principles of Bauhaus production (Dessau)', in Ulrich Conrads (ed) *Programs and Manifestoes on 20th-Century Architecture*, MIT Press (Cambridge, Mass), 1971, p 95. Gropius extends Loos's argument for the unadorned suit as a modern exemplar.

2. Gropius, op cit, p 96.

3. Howard Raggatt, 'NOTNESS: operations and strategies for the fringe', in Leon van Schaik (ed) *Fin de Siecle?*, RMIT/38South (Melbourne), 1993.

4. Dimity Reed (ed) *Tangled Destinies: National Museum of Australia*, Images Publishing Group (Mulgrave, Victoria), 2002. This monograph provides extensive documentation of, and commentary on, the project.

5. Howard Raggatt, 'Once Removed', unpublished interview with Brent Allpress, Melbourne, 1999.

6. Le Corbusier, *The Decorative Art of Today*, trans James I Dunnett, Architectural Press (London), 1987, pp 124–25.

7. Robyn Boyd, *The Australian Ugliness*, Penguin (Sydney), 1963.

8. The federal government will not formally say 'sorry' to the Aboriginal community for past policies that led to children being removed from their parents.

9. Howard Raggatt, 'Once Removed', op cit.

roof, reminiscent of Aldo Rossi's Modena cemetery. The roof plan is drawn from Daniel Libeskind's Berlin Jewish Museum extension.

Cryptic architectural references acknowledge the tragedy of indigenous history that has followed European settlement. A covert contribution to the national debate over reconciliation with Australia's indigenous peoples has been made at a time when the issue has faltered politically.

The interior of the gallery has again been digitally shaped by the Boolean subtraction of a meandering extruded axis. This produces a sinuous linear void figure, evoking the rainbow serpent of the Aboriginal dreamtime.

The gallery exterior is clad with concrete panels precast from CADCAM-generated moulds. The stretched sinuoidal surfaces of the virtual original models impart an exaggerated texture to the concrete. Rendered black, the sciagraphic play of atmospheric shadow effects gives an ambiguous depth and blurred movement to the surfaces, distracting any clear formal focus.

A traditional 'proper' role for ornament has been to make the ordering hierarchies of society legible. For modernists such as Le Corbusier, one of the motivations for rejecting decoration was its conservative social role in maintaining the status quo through 'the promotion of decorum'.[6]

An analogous position was taken by the Melbourne modernist Robyn Boyd in his 1960 book *The Australian Ugliness*. Boyd criticised the Australian suburban cultural desire for 'featurist' ornamental improvements using industrial materials. He also accused his fellow architects of professional propriety and the provision of 'pleasing features'. Ugliness resulted from attempts at decorous beautification, a conservative cultural domestication of modernist prefabrication.[7]

In ARM's work, comfortable cultural proprieties are unsettled by architectural misappropriations. Ornament is suborned. It does not conform to codified grammars of conventional architectural decoration, but rather has a level of operative abstraction that is more open to analysis in terms of its actions: the cutting, moulding, marking and layering of shaped surfaces. Industrial materials are given heightened figurative roles. Cultural meaning or reference is multiple and ambiguous, literally opened up to divergent readings.

For many years, Sydney vagrant Arthur Stace inscribed the word 'Eternity' onto buildings and footpaths across the city. Using packaging software, the conical surfaces of the NMA computer models were unfolded like dressmaking patterns. Stace's 'Eternity' script was overlaid across the complex as an urban supergraphic that exceeds the limits of any one surface.

It is only partially legible as a discontinuous tracery of lines. Text becomes texture.

The exterior polychrome aluminium cladding is embossed with giant Braille that is out of reach to the blind and indecipherable to most sighted visitors. The Braille largely consists of enigmatic colloquial phrases but was also rumoured to address the political impasse over Aboriginal reconciliation.[8]

The ornamental effects produced by the Braille exceed semiotic or formal legibility. Ambiguously scaled, smooth shallow surface indentations cast soft shadows, creating a visual texture inflected with a blurred tactility.

If ornament is 'nothing' in the interiors, a sequence of negative void figures, then across the textured surfaces of the exterior, ornament is everything:

> Everything and nothing because the very tactility of the surfaces seem to supersede the eye to embrace instead a kind of blind insight, like texts read through the finger tips, or like an optical illusion, only able to be appreciated through touch.[9]

ARM makes a virtue of the inherent ambiguity of architecture. Digitally mediated ornament exceeds representation. An unsanctioned space for cultural and architectural aspirations is sought at the limits of legibility where what cannot be clearly articulated might be allowed to surface. ⌂

Ashton Raggatt McDougall,
National Museum of Australia
(NMA), Canberra, 2001

Above
'Eternity' supergraphic and
Boolean subtraction.

Right top
Braille-textured facade.

Right bottom
'Eternity' supergraphic laid out
across the unfolded facades.

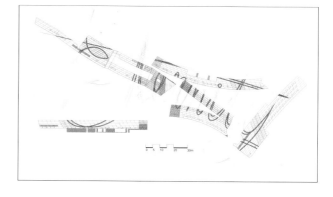

Seduction, Subversion and Predation:
Surface Characteristics

Lyons' On-line Training Centre for Victoria University of Technology is one of the Melbourne practice's most enigmatic works to date. The building's surface with its subtle differences in tone, pattern and texture invites touch, whereas it is in fact flat. **Michael J Ostwald** observes how a variance between surface impression and building form, revealed by the building's folds in the skin that act as sun screens, accentuates an important transfiguration of surface materiality.

In high summer the native grasses in southern Australia turn a reddish-brown shade and in the afternoon sun they cast narrow shadows, like rapid pen-strokes, on the ground. Across such a field of native grass, on the western edge of Victoria University's St Alban's campus near Melbourne, is a curious architectural illusion. From a distance the complex patterns formed by the native grass seem to coalesce into something more uniform. Black triangular shapes, like folds in the earth, punctuate the shift from irregular to regular patterning and signal the presence of something concealed in the landscape adjacent to several university buildings.

As the viewer comes closer it becomes apparent that there is a large, rectilinear structure sitting on the edge of the grasslands, and that this building is richly textured in such a way that from a distance it seems to blend into the site. This closer viewpoint also reveals that the black triangles are shadows cast by folds in the facade to allow indirect light into the building's interior. From this middle vantage point the building is no longer concealed or camouflaged but has now developed a new surface characteristic. While the orthogonal edges are clearly visible the building's skin moirés with each change in position to display subtle differences in tone, pattern and texture that tempt the viewer to approach.

When finally the building is viewed at close range the surface is revealed as a series of regular panels patterned in a richly woven, digital topology. Each panel merges or tiles with those adjacent to it and appears to be perforated, moulded or textured in a way that invites the viewer to run their hand across the building's skin. This act of touching the building – of giving in to its seductive lure – finally reveals a surface that, despite its sensual promise, is perfectly flat. Indeed the folds in the cladding, which screen the windows from harsh sunlight, are detailed to reveal the thinness of the building's skin.

It is this act of peeling back (or folding) the illusory surface to reveal its underside that signals the complicity of the building in a range of strategic architectural bifurcations. When the surface is revealed in this way it becomes the point of inflection between opposing pairs that have already been sensed by the viewer – hidden and revealed, smooth and rough, interior and exterior, structure and ornamentation, and sensible and intelligible. These are canonical binary sets that have been central to historic architectural discourse and politics but which are frequently rejected in contemporary architectural theory and design because they are based on exclusionist rather than inclusionist assumptions.

The zone of contention in any debate surrounding the legitimacy of either of these strategies – the exclusionist and the inclusionist – is the surface or skin of the building. The skin of the On-line Training Centre for Victoria University, by architectural firm Lyons, actively engages the viewers' perceptions and in so doing participates in the debate about the value of conceptual and phenomenological distinctions and the role of bifurcation in architecture.

In his examination of the sociology of religion, Roger Caillois argues for the retention of the natural 'bifurcation of the universe'.[1] For Caillois the preservation of symmetry and opposition is essential to the development of vibrant and fertile social structures. Caillois acknowledges the limitations of binary systems identified in poststructuralist philosophy but insists that such structures are nevertheless useful for social, spatial and ontological reasons. This same issue of bifurcation or division is central to the debate surrounding the concept of 'surface' in much contemporary architecture.

From the earliest architectural treatises the surface of the building has been the inflection point for a range of strategic bifurcations. Whether the division has been between structure and ornamentation or interior and exterior, the amorphous and contested territory of the

surface has provided the line of distinction between one characteristic and another. However, like the poststructuralist philosophers before them, the contemporary architectural avant-garde has been fascinated by the possibility of undermining or destabilising such binary structures. Given the pivotal role played by surface in architectural theory, attempts to critically challenge the political position occupied by surface, on the boundary between different conceptual opposites, have become increasingly provocative.[2]

Architects like Frank Gehry have begun to model the surface of buildings in such a way as to challenge conventional assumptions about the relationship between ornament and structure. Other architects, including Neil Denari and Van Berkel and Bos, have blurred the distinction between exterior and interior by creating continuous surfaces modelled on non-Euclidean Klein bottles and Möbius strips. A third group of architects and designers, including Stephen Perrella, Kas Oosterhuis and dECOi Architects, have experimented with the idea of transforming the entire building into a (hyper)surface structure.

Despite such strategies, the manipulations of the building's surface which most cogently illuminate the philosophically contested territory of the surface are those wherein the form of the building and the impression generated by its skin are most at variance. Lyons is amongst those designers who have occupied this territory most vigorously in recent years.

From its interactive City of Fiction installation for the Venice Biennale in 2000 to its playful and ironic Sunshine Hospital (2001) in Melbourne's western suburbs, Lyons has questioned the role of the surface or skin. Probably the most enigmatic of its recent works is the On-line Training Centre for Victoria University of Technology (2001), which vividly dramatises the way in which the surface of a building may be tactically deployed as a dividing line between different states. In this building the surface is politically active in the sense that it resists simple interpretation without rejecting entirely the role played by the surface in generating distinctions. In this manner it conforms with Caillois's call for necessary bifurcation that acknowledges the limits of binary systems but which values, however obliquely, the clarity they bring to critical analysis. This position is especially evident in Caillois's most 'architectural' work – his investigation of spatial dissimulation and mimesis.

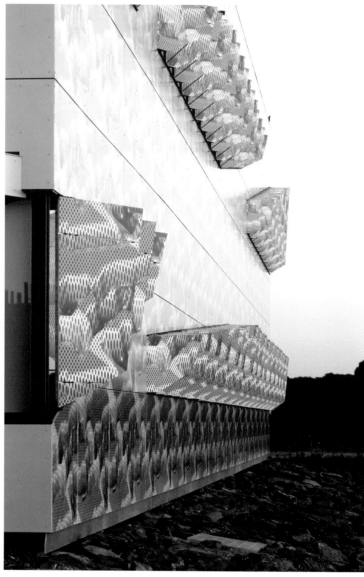

Lyons, Victoria University
On-line Training Centre, St
Albans, Melbourne, 2001

Above left
Open-access computer
precinct with silver interior.

Above right
Sunshade louvres integral
with facade panels.

Caillois argues that '[f]rom whatever side one approaches things, the ultimate problem turns out in the final analysis to be that of distinction: distinctions between the real and the imaginary, between waking and sleeping, [and] between ignorance and knowledge'.[3] The most important distinction Caillois identifies is that between the object and its context or the 'organism and its surroundings'.[4] This dualism is important precisely because 'the tangible experience of separation'[5] is at its most 'immediate' in such binary systems. Yet, he observes, if the distinction between the animal and its environment is so important, what happens when the animal and its environment become indistinguishable? Specifically, what happens when the animal develops surface colouration (homochromy) or implied texture that discourages differentiation between the animal and the environment? This question has also plagued naturalists for more than a century.

In 1862 the English naturalist Henry Bates published his observations of mimicry and the behaviour of butterflies in the *Linnean* journal. Bates proposed that some organisms mimic less palatable or more dangerous organisms for the purpose of avoiding predation. James Huheey

summarises this proposition in the idea that the 'mimic is a sheep in wolf's clothing'.[6] Furthermore, as Wolfgang Wickler notes: 'Bates restricted his definition of mimicry to "resemblance in external appearance, shapes and colours between members of widely distinct families"'.[7] This concept, which is now known as Batesian Mimicry, has been used to explain the reasons why some organisms take on the surface colouration of other organisms, or even their context.

However, Batesian Mimicry is at best only partially supported by empirical evidence. The general problem is that 19th-century naturalists inadvertently assumed that their own logical conception of the universe was shared by animals and insects. They imagined that insects would instinctively realise that camouflage would help increase their rate of survival. The problem with the 'mimicry as defence' argument is that scientific studies have found in the stomachs of birds just as many insects that do mimic inedible forms as those that do not. The Caligo butterfly, which spreads its wings to reveal large eye-shaped markings, may cause a predator to slow its approach but it does not stop the predator.

There is an architectural corollary to this argument about the value of surface characteristics for concealment or subversion.[8] Portmann argues that the animal or insect 'pretends to be something it is not' in order to survive, just as modern armed forces 'use camouflage to protect their ... military installations; the result is proof positive of the defensive value of such techniques'.[9] Wickler disagrees noting that during wars camouflaged buildings 'are also located and destroyed'[10] with great precision. Surface appearances, for animals, insects and architecture, do not guarantee concealment and such mimicry can also be the cause of new forms of predation. As Caillois records: '[t]he case of the Phyllia is even sadder: they browse among themselves, taking each other for real leaves, in such a way that one might accept the idea of a sort of collective masochism leading to mutual homophagy'.[11] All of which suggests that the ultimate purpose of mimicry is not defensive.

For Caillois the essential biological and epistemological problem underlying surface mimicry is that the 'properties of objects are contagious. They change, reverse, combine, and corrupt each other if too great a proximity permits them to interact'.[12] This is much greater than a zoological or entomological issue, for the question of mimicry is not restricted to animals and insects but extends to architecture. Caillois suggests this shift when he proposes that rather than considering these issues under the broad heading of mimicry they should be considered as manifestations of psychasthenia.

According to Caillois, space exerts its own temptation. In the case of mimicry, the breakdown in differentiation between the object and the context is primarily at a surface or visual level. This implies that what is happening in mimicry is essentially 'a disturbance in the perception of space'.[13] The psychological condition that afflicts some people, leading them to believe that they are losing their individual identities and being devoured or subsumed into space, is psychasthenia. Thus Caillois calls the loss of distinction of an object or organism from its surroundings, and the dominance of space over consciousness, legendary psychasthenia. It is the spatial dimension that is most important – when a

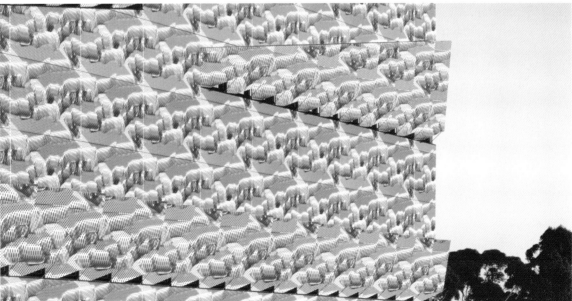

Right top
Sunshade panels control direct sunlight into the computer environment.

Right bottom
West facade in the landscape.

Right
Lyons, Victoria University On-line Training Centre, St Albans, Melbourne, 2001. Digital pattern renders depth optical.

Far right, top
Lyons, Sunshine Hospital, Sunshine, Melbourne, 2001.

Far right, bottom
Lyons, City of Fiction, installation in the Australian Pavilion, Venice Architecture Biennale, 2000.

Notes
1. Roger Caillois, *Man and the Sacred*, Greenwood Press (Westport, CT), 1980, p 63.
2. See Michael J Ostwald and R John Moore, 'Mathematisation or camouflage: between architecture and the applied image', in Richard Blythe and Rory Spence (eds) *Thresholds*, Society of Architectural Historians of Australia and New Zealand (Melbourne), 1999, pp 259–66.
3. Roger Caillois, 'Mimicry and legendary psychasthenia', *October* 31, winter 1984, p 17.
4. Ibid,
5. Ibid,
6. James E Huheey, 'Mathematical models of mimicry', in Lincoln P Brower (ed) *Mimicry and the Evolutionary Process*, University of Chicago Press (Chicago), 1988, p 23.
7. Wolfgang Wickler, *Mimicry in Plants and Animals*, Weidenfeld & Nicolson (London), 1968, p 46.
8. See also Michael J Ostwald, 'Architecture and the evil eye: Coop Himmelblau and the Apotropaic Oculus Invidious', *Interstices*, vol. 5, 2000, pp 56–67.
9. Adolf Portmann, *Animal Camouflage*, University of Michigan (Michigan), 1959, p 7.
10. Wickler, op cit, p 47.
11. Caillois, 'Mimicry and legendary psychasthenia', p 25.
12. Caillois, *Man and the Sacred*, op cit, p 27.
13. Caillois, 'Mimicry and legendary psychasthenia', op cit, p 28.
14. Catherine T Ingraham, 'Animals 2: The problem of distinction (insects for example)', *Assemblage*, 14, April 1991, p 28.

subject is in a perturbed relationship with its context (or space) it suffers a loss of identity. In zoology and entomology this loss of personality through immersion in space is manifested in the form of mimicry and camouflage and is potentially destructive. In the case of architectural surface mimicry, the identity of both the building's skin and the image it adopts can be equally limiting and destructive if it is not well controlled.

Lyons' On-line Training Centre is sheathed in simulations of computer-generated space that beguile the viewer – drawing the viewer closer to the structure until he or she is actually touching its surface. In this sense the building is complicit in promoting the seduction of space through mimicry. For Caillois the danger with this type of mimicry, and the application of images from one object to the surface of another, is that individuation is lost. As Catherine Ingraham argues, mimicry puts 'the distinction between subject and surroundings in danger'.[14]

Assimilation into space typically results in depersonalisation and the loss of distinction, identity and power. Curiously, Lyons' design retains its individuality not because of its distinctive skin, which is admittedly singular, but because of the folds in its surface that act as sun screens. These folds in the facade undermine the surface illusion and unveil its thin materiality in a carefully choreographed manner. They also allow the viewer to see inside the building and to perceive the reality of a space designed for the functional use of computers. It is precisely this act of resistance that prevents the building from succumbing to the over-whelming temptations of digital space, and allows Lyons' design to retain the ability to interrogate the relationships between interior and exterior and structure and ornament that have historically been delineated by surface.

Caillois suggests that distinctions provide a necessary, if inherently flawed, frame of reference. While it may be interesting to argue from a self-referential position, such an inclusive approach that rejects the limitations of a consistent frame of reference is open to criticism for failing to engage with anything other than itself. Similarly, some of the most engaging architectural surfaces are those that acknowledge their role in framing debate, rather than those where a surface is seduced by its own imagery and loses individuation. ∆

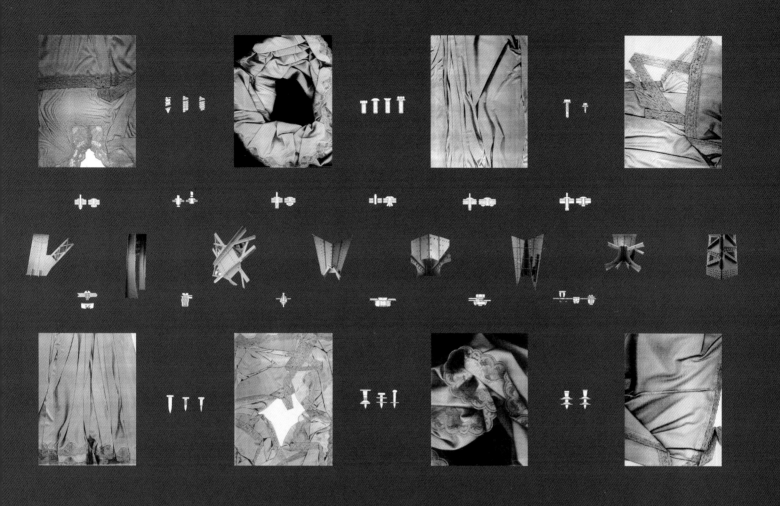

Sewing Surface:
Ground Matters
Beneath the Eiffel Tower

Julieanna Preston suggests that ground (earth) resists being reduced to an abstraction; it is neither a line, coating nor in-between spacer. Her project to fashion a new landscape surface beneath the Eiffel Tower therefore probes the depth of surface. It utilises techniques and practices of sewing to manipulate surface as material having spatial depth – ground as a deep surface.

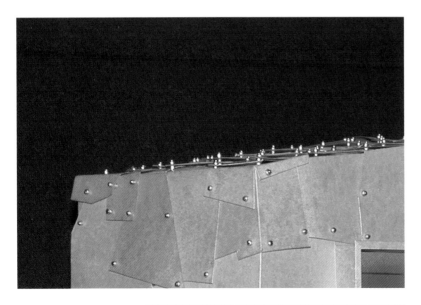

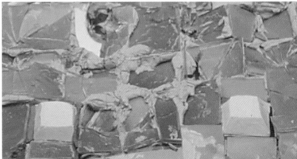

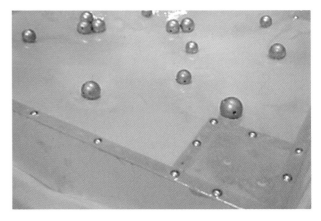

As a prominent figure in the skyline and a popular tourist destination, the Eiffel Tower plays a key role in the contemporary Parisian urban scene. Yet in the monument's shadow lies a landscape surface unable to challenge, accessorise or complement the (em)powered structure. The ground at the feet of the tower lays architecturally fallow. Such observation prompted a proposal to design a new ground surface.

Critics originally dubbed the tower as naked or nude, and questioned its architectural and artistic value. To clothe or clad the Eiffel Tower as though it were a figural body, a statue, casts doubt on its gender and the proprietary boundaries between structure and ornament. Despite its lack of formal enclosure, the Eiffel Tower does not require cladding to extend its cultural value or sustain its pragmatic activities. Even as a remnant of an exhibition, the Eiffel Tower acts as giant scaffolding from which to witness the city. To add an external surface to this frame would be to practise Laugier's architectural principles whereby structure, geometry and rational logic dominate over spatial delineation, interiority, local building methods and material substance.

In contrast, a Semperian model, privileging surface ornament as the first architectural element, envisages the steel skeleton as a clothing prop. Whether a frock or suit, the project imagines a discarded garment/surface falling to the ground as the progenitor to a new topography.[1] The gravity of matter at the ground surface takes on a visible presence because of and despite the ascension of the tower. Informed by conventions of sewing, this metaphoric disrobement generates an architectural design equipped to grapple with theoretical and physical conditions of surface.

The site plan is perhaps the only point from which to witness the extent of the ground's reformation. A resin slip captures the folds of fabric gathered around the tower's feet and its sections describe topographic contours that bound a plaza floor stretched taut by the downward force of the tower's weight. The result of generative material exercises in falling objects, a shattered mosaic matrix comprised of flat shards of concrete, glass and mesh forms a smooth and continuous plaza floor. Contour lines and construction joints between planar tiles conspire to embed the discarded garment within the ground plane. As a result, the focus shifts from the singular object of the tower to a collection of discrete but related fragments in a field.[2] The design proposal reconsiders the location, form and surface articulation of existing elements such as event seating, parking, public toilets, souvenir stands and landscape features. While issues of joining and fabrication are paramount with respect to the project's relation to sewing, these fragments furnish an overall site plan committed to accommodating events and everyday activities among the folds and undulations of a fluid surface – the ground.[3]

Rolled sheets of perforated stainless steel on tiled plinths establish a shifted centre to the tower's imaginary plumb bob. This fragment bravely occupies a space formerly declared as uninhabitable except for a circle of pea gravel. As performance seating, this artificial landscape reflects upon the range of postures between sitting and lying. Informed by sewing techniques, multiple sheets of the same material are gathered so as to increase their surface area and structural capacity.

Readily accessible to people waiting in line to ascend, ablution facilities stand out in full view at the base of each tower leg. Their construction and ornament evolve from a process of selvedge pieces accumulating to form a strong structural shell around the volume of a standardised toilet. Fragmented views of the city framed in the tower's structural matrix fall towards the ground and fold in compliance with common lapped cladding. A toilet block, with all its internal impurities and proprieties, is systematically fabricated by the leftover pieces of another process. Blind rivets hold the plates together and apart to provide natural lighting and ventilation. This detail unifies many irregular pieces as an adorned structural and three-dimensional surface. Like the work of a quality seamstress, the inside seams are as tidy and beautifully crafted as the outside.

Sporting accretions of trinkets on pleated planes of expanded metal mesh wrapped over gigantic cast bobbins, souvenir trolleys collectively congregate as a commercial threshold to the site proper. At night, as the tower is flooded by spotlights, each trolley is securely housed in the deep pockets of a retaining wall, its face disguised as a copper-wire trellis, a variant of vegetal smocking. This fragment capitalises on the social and political circumstances of tourism and the entrepreneurial industries it provokes. The daily rhythm

Right, top and bottom
Event seating.

of vendors 'setting up shop' recalls the temporal and spatial order of markets.

Across the plaza beneath the tower's lacy valance, a row of communication staff monitor crowds and facilitate transmission between the ground and the tower levels. Electronic headdress accessories teeter on their grey-suited bodies as they pivot on pointed tips. Their cast aluminium surface is cold and smooth, a dense hollow shell tracing their origins as muslin needle-casings stuffed with millet seed. No longer the details of seams, the shafts invert the structure/ornament relation by virtue of the exchange and transfer of a casting process. And in a moment of strangeness and familiarity, a voice booms from the staff's head, 'CAN YOU HEAR ME? WHO ARE YOU? WHAT CAN YOU SEE?' The design of this urban fitting reflects practices of pattern making and tailoring. It demonstrates the potential for industrial production to assume unique specificity via small inflections in the fabrication process.

Based on contours of the discarded garment, a constructed landscape replaces duck ponds and tree plantings. To the west, landscaped mounds rise out of the paved plaza floor as a study in bodice work. A network of spatial passages flows between their steep slopes while their crowns privatise a space among a very public urban landscape. To the east, the ground plane has been furrowed as a series of radiating darts. Planted in close-cropped ground cover, the landscape surface directs people and water from the site perimeter to the plaza. Parking canopies hem the site's edge; their fabric membranes funnel atmospheric particles away from the edge of the site and hide vehicles out of view from the tower. Primarily an exercise in structural geometry, the canopy design

Julieanna Preston,
Re-dressing the Eiffel Tower,
2002

Top left
Souvenir trolley model.

Top right
Souvenir trolley extracted from retaining wall.

Bottom
Communication staff.

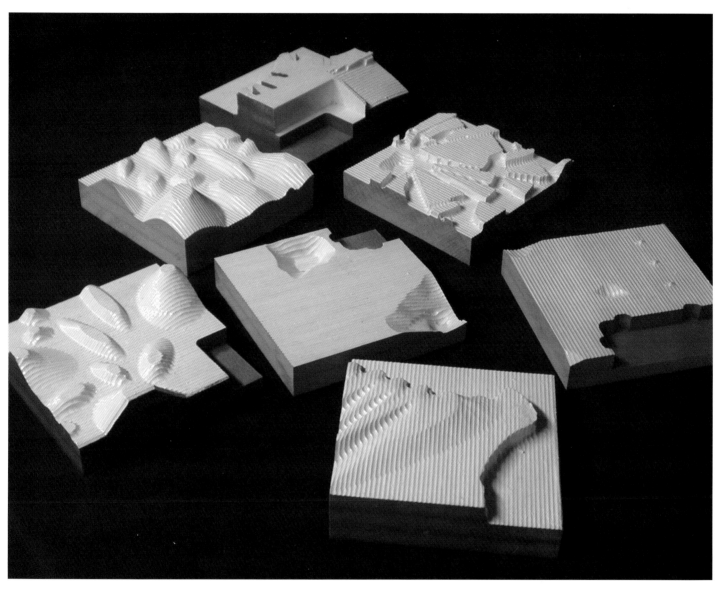

Notes
1. James Corner, 'Eidetic
operations and new
landscapes', in James Corner
and Alan Balfour (eds)
*Recovering Landscape: Essays
in Contemporary Landscape
Architecture*, Princeton
Architectural Press (Princeton,
NJ), 1999, p 159.
2. Omar Calabrese, *Neo-
Baroque: A Sign of the Times*,
Princeton University Press
(Princeton, NJ), 1992, pp 68–90.
3. David Leatherbarrow,
*Uncommon Ground:
Architecture, Technology and
Topography*, MIT Press
(Cambridge, Mass), 2000, p 129.
4. Avrum Stroll, *Surfaces*,
University of Minnesota Press
(Minneapolis), 1988, pp 39–68.

Above
CNC-generated surface models.

presents surface as a two-sided condition: the
underside space is dabbled with elliptical
projections of colour and strewn with lashing
hardware, and the upper face is a smooth
membrane stretched across a supportive frame.

Pursuance of design as a condition of
articulating surface enlists thinking and making
processes that operate between and across
that which is conceptual and abstract and that
which is concrete and physical. In this project,
techniques and practices of sewing have
exposed strategies of manipulating surface
as a material and three-dimensional substance
intimately involved with the production of public
landscape, urban fittings and spatial interiors.
While, as a philosopher, Avrum Stroll rigorously
examines surface as a boundary or limit, the
architectural issue is the depth of surface as
a tangible aspect of body, time and space.[4]

The limit of Stroll's abstraction is witnessed in
the everyday objects he uses to demonstrate his
theoretical models of surface. An apple, marble
and table are objects we can grasp.

The physicality of ground is no less corporeal:
it is the relatively stable matter covering the earth, a
substance that nourishes plant growth and a medium
in and on which we build. Despite its prolific presence,
it eludes definition as a singular condition or model
of surface. Just as in Stroll's discussion about lakes
or mountains, or even people, ground is an entity that
resists being reduced to abstraction. The ground is not
a line, a coating nor a nonexistent in-between spacer.
Its boundaries are hypothetical and its limits are
construed for the convenience of measurement and
political ownership. In the case of this design project,
an urban landscape was fabricated and fitted by
multiple scales of detail that reveal surface as having
spatial and material depth. Ground is a deep surface. ∆

Surface:
Architecture's Expanded Field

Prompted by her daily walks around Ngargee, Wood Marsh Architects' contemporary arts space in Melbourne, **Karen Burns** takes a self-reflexive journey around surface. This invites a rethinking of the role and power of surface, which necessitates invoking its others phantasms – such as interior, form and structure – which underlie our very definitions of surface.

Close to my work place a building nears completion. Almost every weekday I walk beside the massive surfaces of the Australian Centre for Contemporary Art (ACCA). I circle the perimeter of the building and track its towering, evanescent sides. Great planes of red-brown, clotted, rusting steel dig their edges into the yellow ochre dirt, poised to bisect the earth. ACCA's plinth is barely visible. A tiny black rim is tucked beneath its thick auburn sheets.

Currently the building presses the sandy ground-soil like a classic, late-modernist sculpture.[1] Monumental in scale, the building produces a compelling magnetic field, pushing the viewer backwards to contemplate the work within a surrounding ground. A space seems to have cleared around ACCA, releasing an 'expanded field' of viewing. In front of the building, ground surface acts as plinth, boundary and field of vision.[2] No ambiguity troubles the definitive material edges of this architecture. It is a cracked, rusting fort of heavy, hard-edged steel. You might knock against it and hear sound echoing deep within an underground cavern. However, the earth seems a necessary part of the completed building. Ground and work are distinct yet bound together in tension.

This ineluctable connection amongst distinct component elements generates a certain degree of surface activity. Pressure appears amongst the individual parts. Rising planes fold almost imperceptibly to form a slight 'v', a minor inward ripple on the building's northeastern edge. On the northwest side where the building sits against an arching freeway, the plane parts to reveal a building composed of a series of planes, in part wrapped over each other. On the southwestern side, the plane cranks and inverts to a deep 'v'. Here the tension between the resolutely flat surface of monumental sheets of steel and the inward bend where the surfaces meet provides the most dramatic suggestion of imperceptible forces at work. Within the viewer, questions arise. Is there an elsewhere, another site, perhaps an interior point exerting and registering pressure upon these exterior surfaces?

Interior is both located and displaced in this project. ACCA literalises and enacts a form of 'contemporary surface consciousness'.[3] Of course this building contains an interior. It houses galleries, offices, rehearsal rooms, storage and performance spaces. ACCA undertakes the traditional work of architecture: sheltering and defining a series of enclosed volumes. It sets boundaries and defines limits. It may also signify other interiors. As a witty colleague of mine observed, the shifting ground beneath the building forms another unbidden interior to this project.

ACCA stands beside the ventilation tower of a subterranean freeway tunnel. The tunnel has experienced a series of technical obstacles, cracking and leaking water into its sealed interior. The earth, nature, that apparent other to culture stealthily enacts its revenge on constructed work. An unintended irony is invoked by this building's folded and fractured exteriors. But then so many contemporary architectural forms replicate the movement of subliminal below-ground activity. In the words of this issue's guest-editor:

Earthquakes and lava flows no longer crack or cover 'the skin of the earth' but reveal its substance as 'live', animate and complex. Such natural events of surface instability show themselves to be analogous, associative or parallel locations/ indicators for realisation of architectural surface.[4]

Beyond the metaphoric or imitative function of these analogies what desire invests our reliance on these models of 'natural' events?

Perhaps the interior has not disappeared but registers its power as a motive force. The metaphor of geological slippage is pertinent. 'Natural' formations such as geological events offer a metaphor and model of surface instability to be invoked and imitated by architecture. Geological metaphor is not a reflection of a prior event but a form of poetic ornament engaged in intellectual and material work. Architectural metaphor is a mimicry or enactment of a certain philosophical labour. An editor of an earlier issue of *Architectural Design* devoted to 'hypersurface architecture' observed: 'Hypersurface is a reconsideration of often dichotomous relationships existing in the environment'.[5] These dichotomies might be metaphorically realised as different geological planes representing distinct philosophical categories. One plane may represent surface, the other plane represents an interior, or the layers signify other dualistic terms such as form/ structure. Slippage, fractures and fissures warp existing binary distinctions. Hairline fractures, fault lines or the deeper abyss trace the force of movement between the categories and establish connections hitherto kept distinct or invisible. Geological activity provides a certain literalisation of a series of moves and strategies within critical theory activity. Architectural philosophy may be one interior force powering away here.

Even as we seek to erase or press the limits of one category it remains tied to its silent twin. How can we rethink the role and power of surface without invoking its others, those phantasms – interior, form and structure – the presence of which structures the definition of surface? If hypersurface architecture seeks to question or displace its ground it must of course invoke that very ground. Surface registers as surface only as a distinction among other terms. No wonder so much critical and material work to place categories under erasure results in slippage and fracture amongst categories and within material built surfaces. Slippage applies. The banished of course have an obstinate habit of returning. Their absence results in a palpable presence of traces: ghosts of past architectures. So we must negotiate the phantasm of these other interiors: interior, form, structure. The reformation of surface critically depends on the ground, on that ineluctable tension between the work and its other or elsewhere.

The other, the elsewhere, some other interior exterior to this one, hovers over and haunts contemporary architecture. ACCA's expanded field generates a ground surface of earth as plinth, boundary and viewing field for the building. An architectural surface transforms surrounding surfaces through its act of construction. On one level the massive form of

Minifie/Nixon Architects (Paul
Minifie and Fiona Nixon)
extension to the union and
library buildings, Victorian
College of the Arts (under
construction, due for
completion 2003)

Opposite
View from northwest.

Above
West elevation.

the building would seem to assert its objecthood and yet the work's legibility depends on its expanded field. Unsurprisingly ACCA resonates with the influence of the late 1960s minimalist sculptors, in particular Richard Serra. Sculpture's transformation of Greenburgian modernism's obsession with the zero surface of painting – flat, flat, flat – into an insistence on the object hood of the work resulted in a paradoxical emphasis on surface and an extended sense of the work's surface as the surrounding ground. Contemporary architectural surface is in part a renunciation of architecture's isolated-object status. Instead architecture resides within a network.

Architecture has become a site of interconnection. Different terms, all signifying a larger system of interdependence, circulate in contemporary architectural discourse: pattern, system, process, network, feedback loop, software programs, mathematical models mapping complex patterns and events. A supervening system commonly defines these terms. Sometimes the system's task is to systematise things that apparently fall outside it, things that would seem to be exterior to its regulated structure, such as quantifiable uncertainty or the 'voronoi' concept that models local contingency. Minifie/Nixon, another Melbourne architectural firm, used the voronoi system to generate the facade pattern of a building currently under construction: the library, computer laboratory and residence of the Centre for Ideas at the Victorian College of

the Arts. Architecture's place within a larger system has an established history. Following the construction of the modernist city in the 19th century, buildings were integrated into a city circuit. Sewerage, electricity, water and, later, telephone connections established architecture's place within the urban network. What distinguishes contemporary architecture is not merely the new network opportunities of contemporary electronic technologies but architecture's desire to reflexively represent this networked structure within itself, within the philosophical or ontological interior of architectural design.

Surface renders these networked or system connections visible. Surface screens or projects the visualisation of these ideas. The facade of Minifie/Nixon's building transposes the voronoi concept into a three-dimensional realisation. Metallic, bronzed panels are buttoned by a series of localised centres: sheathed windows and oversized screws quilting the surface plane. These baroque undulations reverberate with vague uncanny ease. The building's designer observed that the voronoi system privileges the local event.[6] If one centre is moved all the others must follow. Network connections are vulnerable to flow-on effects from events arising elsewhere. This facade halts the voronoi system and renders it static. In one sense this is architecture's apparent limitation and its source of social power. A building grounds and limits and stabilises the world's flux. It temporarily presents the appearance of permanence and continuity. Spectators release architecture's temporal life, producing mutability and contingency. Light catches the patina of bronzed panels on Minifie/Nixon's building. Surface shifts, warping under the refraction of luminosity, generating change amongst

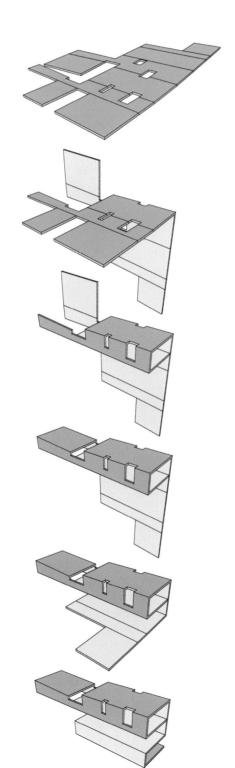

Minifie/Nixon Architects (Paul
Minifie and Fiona Nixon)
extension to the union and
library buildings, Victorian
College of the Arts

Above
Voronoi diagram.

BKK Architects (Tim Black,
Julian Kosloff and Simon
Knott) Wrap House,
Melbourne (under
construction, due for
completion 2003)

Right
Folding diagram model.

Opposite
Floor plans.

the triangulation of facade, viewer and field of vision.
Human vision is notoriously unreliable and susceptible
to optical illusion and 'aberrant' phenomena. The
reception of information on the surface of the human
retina transforms the condition of the object.

Vision is a temporal phenomenon. Temporality has
entered architectural design and discourse at a moment
when time-based representational techniques such as
video and computer-modelling sequences dominate
architectural presentation and design methods. John
Ruskin, that crusty, eccentric Englishman of letters,
also wrote about architecture at a point when the world
was in flux, at that moment we now name as
modernism. In his magnum opus, *The Stones of Venice*,
he noted of the Basilica San Marco:

> No amount of illustration or eulogium would be
> enough to make the reader understand the
> perfect beauty of the thing itself, as the sun steals
> from interstice to interstice of its marble veil, and
> touches with the white lustre of its rays at midday
> the pointed leaves of thirsty lilies.[7]

Ruskin's assertion of vision's contingency under the
sign of the semitransparent veil is worth revisiting.
Surface is not a blank tabula rasa, a projection space
for the eye or the sun. The veil signifies active and
engaged representation; the constructed, temporal
nature of architectural culture and vision. One thing
we might say about the current attention to surface is
that the discourse on surface manifests the operations
of representation.

A veil does not merely lay one surface over another
but transforms and filters the very material that seems
to be its raw substance. The veil was enshrined as a
powerful sign within European art. In the genre of the
nude the veil's traditional gesture of modesty clothed
the body and accentuated the smooth patina of
luscious, naked flesh. It exposed what it sought to hide.
Another fold rippled within the veil. What the veil
apparently drew attention to, what it veiled, was not
necessarily another surface but the interior conditions
of representation. As T J Clark has persuasively argued,
something more remains suppressed by the nude's veil
and its veiled flesh, something invisible and largely
unspoken: eroticism, desire and power.[8]

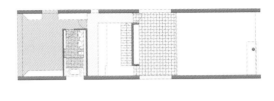

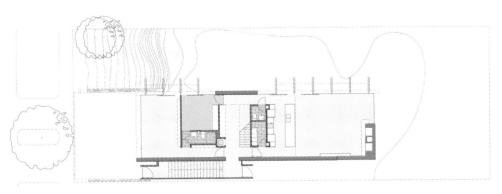

Notes

1. Of course we could argue about the nomenclature. What I describe as late modernist, Rosalind Krauss would describe as postmodern. See Rosalind Krauss, 'Sculpture in the expanded field', in *The Originality of the Avant-Garde and Other Modernist Myths*, MIT Press (Cambridge, Mass, and London), 1985, pp 276–90.

2. Ibid, p 284.

3. Mark Taylor, 'Editor's Brief', personal communication, 14 February 2002.

4. Ibid.

5. Stephen Perrella, 'Hypersurface theory: Architecture culture', in Stephen Perrella (ed) 'Hypersurface architecture', *Architectural Design*, vol 68, no 5/6, May/June 1998, p 8.

6. Interview with Paul Minifie, 15 August 2002.

7. Edward Tyas Cook and Alexander Wedderburn (eds) *The Library Edition: The Works of John Ruskin*, vol 10, 'The Stones of Venice' by John Ruskin, George Allen (London), 1903, p 165.

8. T J Clark, *The Painting of Modern Life*, Thames and Hudson (London), 1985, pp 131–46.

9. Here I am paraphrasing and reversing Avital Ronnell's observation on the unconscious. She observes that the unconscious is 'not a hidden, virtual or potential self-practice but an apparatus that sends out delegates, representatives, proxies, phone messages and obscene phone calls taken but not essentially put through, often missing their mark'. See Avital Ronnell, *The Telephone Book: Technology, Schizophrenia, Electric Space*, University of Nebraska Press (Lincoln, Nebraska, and London), 1989, p 85.

The discourse of the nude was veiled by high cultural aspirations. Its lascivious possibilities were concealed beneath the traditional claims of aesthetics and highbrow narratives of classical legends and historical events. Girlie pix were furtively disguised and slipped between the prim covers of art. The nude suppressed and displaced the erotic investment of its producers: the painters and spectators. Its surfaces stimulated, enacted and energised sexual desire. These forces and power relations were never explicitly located on the naked surface of the picture, but were mobilised around and outside the image in the moment of spectatorship, theorisation and consumption.

The veil is paralleled in contemporary architecture. The current discourse on surface gestures towards a kind of hypervisibility. We attend to visible surface. Surface and its networks or other interlocutors are tangled skeins, however, rather than immediately consumed planes of images and meanings. The relations between things trouble our desire for visibility. Architects, critics and spectators stake claim on the legible nature of surface meaning, but these surfaces are also the delegates, representatives, proxies, phone messages, misplaced calls of other culturally invested interiors: the discourse of authorship, the desire for legibility and other social and political formations.[9]

Surface may not be the place of all the hype, but an indication of hidden others and hidden interiors. Our renewed attention to architectural surface is accompanied by a strong sense of other sites: the network, category slippage, a revisioning of the ground plane. The expanded field of architecture is only in part materially and symbolically represented in continuous built surfaces such as walls that become ground planes and facades that represent larger ordering systems. Surface manifests and veils the tension between what can be absolutely seen or represented and what remains hidden.

Signs of this tension are signalled and traced rather than explicitly represented and exposed. It may be enough to allude to, rather than explicate, the friction between a site and its larger network/category/ terminology/information system. In BKK's Wrap House, under construction in Melbourne, the undulating line inscribed in the landscape of the ground plan evokes the veil as a clear sign, at least in plan form. The 'wrapped' exterior surfaces are more literal depictions of surface as 'wrap'. Using two signs and rendering one, the wrap, more visible than the other, allows one site to explore the shifting, possible meanings of the term 'surface', where the literal and the trace ghost each other. Inscriptions of surface upon different surfaces – facade and ground – materialise different registrations of surface in each act of building. Surface is, of course, surfaces, not a unitary object but a calibration of different possibilities. Ground of some kind – the earth's plane, the network and architecture's interior categories under erasure – is necessary for renewed architectural surface activity. Architecture is not merely a surface analogous to the earth's surface but our highly constructed cultural interior: a site, a sheet, where seismic markings, great and small, trace but do not necessarily specify or control ineluctable connections and reverberations. ⚙

Brent Allpress is the Architecture Program Director at the Royal Melbourne Institute of Technology in Melbourne, Australia. He is also the Melbourne contributing editor to *Monument*. He was born and educated in Auckland, New Zealand, and completed a Bachelor of Architecture (Hons) and Masters of Architecture at the University of Auckland. He is currently undertaking PhD research on the contemporary role of ornament.

Dr Karen Burns teaches at the Centre for Ideas at the Victorian College of the Arts in Melbourne. Her essays have been published in *Assemblage* and the collections *Desiring Practices* and *Post Colonial Spaces*. She is currently investigating the relations between photography, visuality and architectural design in the 1840s and 1850s.

Professor Mark Burry is a practising architect and recently took up a position at RMIT University in Melbourne, Australia, as Professor of Innovation (Spatial Information Architecture). Previously he held the chair in architecture and building at Deakin University for five years. He has published internationally on two main themes: the life and work of the architect Antonio Gaudí in Barcelona, and putting theory into practice with regard to 'challenging' architecture. He has also published widely on broader issues of design, construction and the use of computers in design theory and practice.

Bernard Cache is the leading principal of the Paris-based design and software company Objectile, which he founded in 1996 with Patrick Beaucé and Jean-Louis Jammot. Cache has acted as a senior consultant in major strategic studies on image telecommunications and digital television for companies such as Philips, Canal Plus and France Telecom. Published internationally, he has written widely on communication policy and economics as well as architecture. He has most recently held academic appointments as Associate Professor of Architectural Design and Computing at the University of Toronto, Visiting Professor at the Universidad Internacional de Catalunya, and Visiting Professor at the School of Architecture, UCLA.

Hans Frei studied architecture at the Swiss Institute of Technology (ETH), where he completed his doctoral dissertation entitled 'Max Bill as Architect'. He has practised as an architect in Zurich, and since 1996 has been Professor of Architectural Theory and Design at the University of Kassel, Germany.

Victoria Interrante is a McKnight Land-Grant Assistant Professor in the Department of Computer Science and Engineering at the University of Minnesota. Her research focuses on the application of insights from visual perception, art and illustration to the design and implementation of more effective techniques for visualising data.

Horst Kiechle holds Masters degrees in Civil Engineering from the University of Karlsruhe, Germany, and in Fine Arts from the University of New South Wales, Australia. He was the inaugural 'Artist in Residence' at the CSIRO, Australia, and has held guest research positions at GMD, Germany, and Interactive Institute, Sweden.

Professor Michael Ostwald is Dean of Architecture and Head of the School of Architecture and the Built Environment at the University of Newcastle, Australia. He has written extensively about the relationship between architecture, geometry and philosophy.

Julieanna Preston is an architectural designer working and living in Wellington, New Zealand. Under the auspices of 'Building Arts Practice' her works have been presented, exhibited and published internationally. These works find various forms such as installations, full-scale construction, design competitions and speculative research-by-design projects.

Timothy M Rohan is an assistant professor of architectural history at the University of Massachusetts, Amherst, US. He has contributed articles to *Grey Room*, *Casabella* and some edited collections.

Mark Taylor is a senior lecturer at Victoria University Wellington, New Zealand. He has recently co-authored *Moments of Resistance* (Sydney, Arcadia Press), and is currently researching gender and 19th-century architectural theory..

Sarah Treadwell is a senior lecturer at the School of Architecture, University of Auckland, New Zealand. Her research considers architectural images, weather and colonial representations.

Michael Trudgeon is the principal designer with Crowd Productions P/L, a Melbourne-based multidisciplinary design practice engaged in research and in developing scenarios for the use of new technologies in industrial design and architecture.

Peter Wood is a lecturer in architectural theory at Victoria University Wellington, New Zealand. Currently his research is concerned with the impact of technological change on the traditional value systems of architectural production.

94+   Interior Eye:
Deluxe Apartments in the Sky
Craig Kellogg

97+   Practice Profile:
Kathryn Findlay of Ushida Findlay
Neil Spiller

103+   Building Profile:
Federation Square, Melbourne
Jeremy Melvin

110+   Engineering Exegesis:
Blurring the Lines: Mediating between
analogue and digital skill sets   *Mark Burry*

119+   Highlights from Wiley Academy
Jane Peyton

120+   Congratulations to Jayne Merkel
Helen Castle

122+   Invisibly Informal   *Lucy Bullivant*

126+   Site Lines
Building Exploratory
Hannah Ford

In densely developed cities like New York, penthouse apartments are the ultimate expression of personal privilege. Floating high above the fray, their designers are often free to ignore both contextual and stylistic constraints. **Craig Kellogg** introduces the Manhattan partnership of Rogers Marvel Architects, a young modernist practice. Working for a well-heeled clientele, the firm is gaining a reputation for producing those eyries that look down upon the rest of us.

Deluxe Apartments in the Sky

Below left
Downstairs, the owners have personalised what was formerly the top floor
of the building with framed children's art and wallpaper in a vintage pattern.

Below right
The view from the mezzanine of the penthouse addition shows the living area below.
Windows face the spectacular Midtown Manhattan skyline. The long, narrow shape
of the addition matches the footprint of the base building, a town house.

The noble brownstone street facade of Beethoven Hall has been painted an anonymous industrial grey, and plain steel doors are fitted into the old entry archway where something nicer clearly belongs. The large windows hint at a history of better days in the neighbourhood where the building sits. (Side streets off the Bowery are again fashionable, and sometimes festive in patches.) But, even when judged according to the prevailing standards of Manhattan's Lower East Side, where squalor is highly regarded as a mark of authenticity, Beethoven Hall is more or less a blight. Nevertheless, the building is worth another look, not least because of the clever camouflage it affords its occupants. Generous, open interiors that were once configured as a television studio have been divided into a series of live-work artists' lofts by Rogers Marvel Architects. Surmounting the existing structure is the same architects' splashy penthouse addition, a big international-style box with smooth new walls and ceilings more than 20 feet high.

Penthouses are not precisely an interior type. Building them usually requires a new structure, roof and (often) landscape – just as do houses in suburbia. But because penthouses are tucked mostly out of sight on roof tops they afford a unique

opportunity for architects to design from the inside out, barely caring about the consequences to exterior elevations. Conceptually the conceit is that the base building is a plain pedestal. This is what liberates designers, giving them the licence to experiment boldly with fundamentals of scale and style.

Living space added on the roof of Beethoven Hall completely fills the allowable zoning envelope. So, as in many New York penthouses, the scale is astonishing. The double-height grand salon with polished concrete floors is used primarily for entertaining guests. (Four bedrooms and other intimate everyday spaces for the family of five are located just downstairs in what was formerly the top floor of the existing structure, where the ceilings are lower.) Walls of windows and glass doors allow skyline views of the city and access to the four outdoor 'rooms' – terraces where pavers, plants in pots and outdoor furniture comprise the 'landscaping'. Indoors, the domestic landscape of mid-century furniture and Tibetan carpets is divided by low, built-in mahogany credenzas with marble tops.

Below
At the top of the stairs, marble-topped credenzas serve as low walls that zone the penthouse addition. The wall-mounted light box is one of a number of details throughout the apartment that were inspired by the art of Piet Mondrian.

Below top
Exterior view of penthouse interiors on previous pages.

Below bottom
Paul Rudolph penthouse.

Gotham Penthouse Primer

Tourists in Manhattan sometimes get their most revealing glimpses of the island's penthouses through the scratched plastic windows of commercial jetliners flying overhead. Since there are no roads in Manhattan, there aren't really any roadsides. By contrast, roof-top development can be hard to spot from street level, since city regulations usually dictate that new construction be invisible to pedestrians. Notable exceptions include penthouses that predate the regulations. The Paul Rudolph apartment is a masterpiece of constructivism that Rudolph heaped onto the roof of a staid town house on the East Side. Its interiors continue his experiments with the sheer, cascading multilevel spaces that obsessed him throughout his tumultuous career. Important newer examples integrate penthouses into an overall architectural scheme. Perhaps the most outstanding is the 1975 Galleria apartment building, on 57th Street between Park and Lexington avenues, which makes a similarly bold contribution to the Manhattan skyline by wearing its penthouse like a Corbusian crown.

Furnishings were chosen by trendy New York dealer and decorator Steven Sclaroff, an acquaintance of the clients who himself went to architecture school. Despite the prominence and provenance of the pieces, they do not overshadow the decorative details supplied by Rogers Marvel. The firm specified all of the interior architectural finishes, and the motif is mostly Mondrian. That artist's characteristic grids are expressed in the pattern of window mullions, in the milky light-boxes that incorporate the odd-coloured panel and in the asymmetries of elements such as the fireplace surround.

The strong geometries and white volumes of the interiors are not unlike those of the Kate Spade handbag stores designed by Rogers Marvel. (One of the penthouse owners is, unsurprisingly, a Kate Spade executive.) And the same architects are currently fortunate to be engaged with projects for two other well-heeled clients: a residence for a textiles designer and a home-and-studio for a sculptor. Both mix interior and exterior space, combining the renovated top floor or floors of a hardworking existing building with something new and truly grand above. Though not large by the standards of America's new suburban megamansions, they are large enough to impress. For the select class of New Yorkers with both the means and the will, it seems a custom penthouse is the perfect Downtown pied-à-terre. ᴪ

Below
Poolhouse interior, 2001.

Kathryn Findlay of Ushida Findlay

Neil Spiller reviews the work of Kathryn Findlay as she reaches a watershed in her career. After a long period in Japan, she has returned to the UK only to mop up some of the most interesting design opportunities. As a practice, Ushida Findlay continues to distinguish itself through the artisan quality of its designs and Findlay's particular ability to manipulate materials while also combining the seemingly incompatible. Can the office, however, resist the temptation to expand?

Below
Grafton New Hall
The Royal Institute of British Architects launched an invited competition in March 2001 for a new modern country house – Grafton New Hall. The site for the 25,000-square-foot house is on a 114-acre country estate in south Cheshire. The estate dates back to Roman times, and was known since the 13th century as the manor of Grafton. In the early 17th century, Grafton Hall was built on this site. The house fell into disrepair in the 20th century and was demolished in 1963. Ushida Findlay's proposal is a 21st-century vision for modern country living – a contextural yet sustainable and energy-efficient approach to building. Externally, the design for Grafton New Hall is distinctive and sympathetic to the character of the

surrounding woodland. It will extend like fingers out into the low-lying surrounding meadow creating a series of ridges and furrows, which will reflect, enhance and frame the natural contours of the medieval landscape and allow the building's scale, orientation and mass to be informed by the location. Internally, too, the design is nature-orientated. It is a clear, fanning spiral, feathering at the edges. The orientation of Grafton New Hall is such that the pattern of daily activity can loosely follow the path of the sun whilst also providing effective shade.

Below left
Kathryn as the depressed Virgin Mary.

As I sit in Findlay's packed studio she shows me a slide of her face superimposed on the Virgin Mary, the one that supports Christ as part of Michelangelo's Pietà, which is displayed in St Peter's Cathedral in Rome. It is a strangely disturbing image. Findlay happily said she made it a few years ago when she was depressed one day. Findlay, one would guess, has little to be depressed about these days – she is the talk of London town. In the short time since she returned to London, after a long domicile in Japan, she has hoovered up some of the most interesting architectural opportunities. She wins design competitions with displays of surprising formal dexterity yet these projects have also a contextual quality despite her sometimes formal conceits.

Each win is wilder than the previous one, and she seems not to worry about what might be unachievable later on due to economic, pragmatic and time constraints. She seems to greet every problem happily as a creative opportunity. Compromise doesn't seem to be too prominent in her architectural lexicon. This is not to imply that her work is wrapped up in its own little

world; to the contrary, every project starts from the first principles of the peculiar phenomenology of its site. Findlay then seeks to accommodate, accentuate and elucidate these disparate demands until the form starts to suggest itself. Like most architects, certain geometries and certain complex configurations cause her aesthetic enjoyment, and this is the key to her architectural syntax. But we are getting in front of ourselves.

Findlay is an alumna of the Architectural Association (AA), another product of the AA's halcyon days (late 1970s and 1980s). She talks particularly fondly of architectural cyberneticist Ranulph Glanville. Design/form-wise, she was perhaps mostly steered by Christine Hawley, Leon van Schaik and the ubiquitous Peter Cook during this heady period. After graduation she developed a fascination with all things Japanese, and did a stint in Arata Isozaki's office. She met her future husband, Eisaku Ushida, there. It was their separation that prompted her return to London a few years ago.

The office she established in London has accumulated
an impressive array of recent graduates with surprising and
original preoccupations and tastes. There is certainly no
shortage of youthful vision and talent in the Findlay office.
Findlay is an external examiner at the Bartlett School and
likes to keep an eye on some of the many talented young
architects that pass through its doors – if I was just fully
entering the profession she would be on my list.

When we met to discuss this practice profile she talked
of 'the interstitial – the space between, where things happen'.
This 'space' manifests itself as the surprising aesthetic and
pragmatic juxtapositions that occur almost by accident,
when she decides to thatch a glass poolhouse for example,
punctuating the ridge of the roof with modern roof lights
and planting a few scrubs up there. Another example is her
contemporary stately home that is basically barrel-vaulted
stone fingers dug half in and half out of the site – the
distinction between in and out artfully blurred. She also
likened this process of the 'interstitial' as happening when

insulation foam is injected into a cavity and it finds its
way out of all the little fissures, blobbing out into a
whole new previously unconceived landscape. This
approach of combining what at first might be seen as
incompatible is plain to see in the Soft and Hairy House
built in Japan. These strange, otherworldly houses
would not be conspicuous on the set of Roger Vadim's
1968 film *Barbarella*, and they oddly predict many of
the stylistic predilections of some of the new young
things lurking about today.

It takes steely determination to build architectures
like Findlay's, and I sense that under her modest,
relaxed facade is a steely willpower and determination
few will mess with.

Like Ben Nicholson (an AA contemporary) but for
different reasons, Findlay's work can be read as a
search for a different definition of the expressions
'house' and 'home'. The house is the microcosm of
architecture, in effect architecture's fundamental atom.

Below
Soft and Hairy House and Truss Wall House
The Soft and Hairy House (1994) (below) and Truss Wall House (1993) (opposite) illustrate the beginning of Ushida Findlay's preoccupations with organic, wrapped-around form, the firm's penchant for the 'berming' of landscape over parts of its buildings and its ability to transcend the usual protocols of roof, wall and floor. These works, done while Kathryn Findlay was still

calling Japan 'home', had a wide resonance and impact across the world. Anyone who really cared about the development of architecture watched the flowering of these unusual little gems with a warm twinkle in the corner of the eye.

Findlay's evolving house preoccupations, starting with the Japanese houses and continuing through the new country house referred to as Grafton and other newer designs, as yet unpublishable due to her client's wish for anonymity, lead one to think of Fredrick Kiesler's Endless House projects.

Kiesler's Endless programmes were spurred on by his radical dislike of the tyranny of the modernist box propagated by the purveyors of the international style. Likewise, Findlay is battling the forces of mediocrity and the lacuna of creative thought exhibited by money-grabbing reactionary house-builders across the world. Kiesler's Endless work was first exhibited in Vienna in 1924, but the preoccupations of 'endlessness' informed his whole career and culminated in his 1953–59 project for the Endless House. Its polemic aims were to 'break the cube-prison tradition, to liberate space into galaxies of disclosed spaces, to invent a special construction system – the shell in continuous tension, to eliminate the distinction between floor, wall and ceiling of the box'.[1] To top this, the Endless House was also conceived by Kiesler as a 'Colour Clock'; at different times of the day the house, aided by the differing positions of the sun, internally radiated different coloured light, the time of day becoming abundantly clear just by the hue of the house's internal surfaces. The end result was a house design with the rough geometry of a cluster of slightly cracked eggs.

Findlay is not unfamiliar with all these aspirations for contemporary living. Like Kiesler, she sees the city as unnecessarily divided or truncated from the country. Both Findlay and Kiesler search in their very different ways for methods to eradicate this arbitrary distinction. Again like Kiesler, Findlay sees contemporary living as 'elastic' – the contemporary dwelling needs to accommodate an almost spiritual openness and joy in living life. Kiesler attempted to describe this quality as 'the elasticity of building adequate to the elasticity of living'.[2]

Findlay's main tactic in attempting to disengage the country–city dichotomy, the natural and artificial, the husbanded and the self-sown, the sleek and the rough, is the notion of material 'flow'. Materials seem

to almost liquidly flow over, between and through her work, whether they are man-made or biological. This quality creates an 'endless' aesthetic of her own. As well as the floor and wall not being differentiated, the inside and the outside are seldomly simply defined, and the landscape and its myriad of drivers and devices are fully integrated into the buildings. This all serves to give a synaesthetic feeling seldom experienced, all mixed up with feminine guile.

Findlay's work is also about seeing the familiar in a previously unimagined way. The Situationists used this notion polemically and termed it *detournement* – art created from diverting aesthetic elements. Findlay is certainly less political than the Situationists, yet she is just as able to subvert an idea, construction technique or material to her advantage and this tactic is always central to her most successful sensual work. She also has some nicely powerful friends who are always willing to indulge her aspirations. She seems to talk the language of architects but is capable of communicating with developers, entrepreneurs and planners – no visionary-genius exclusivity for her. One suspects the Kathryn Findlay story is far from over, and in fact that it has only just begun.

One question will soon need to be answered. Will Findlay be able to maintain the same artisan quality of her practice as it expands? This expansion has caused many a lithe practice to incorporate into its internal structure all manner of corporate hierarchies and 'quality assurance' protocols, that have served to obscure good work in the vapour trails of arcane bureaucracy and produce work that has no merit but to bulk up the monthly fee-invoicing totals as the number of baby birds that need to be fed increases. This has been, historically, a catch 22 situation that has been the artistic death of many architects. I for one certainly hope she doesn't fall prey to this, the nastiest downside to success. Thankfully she is showing no sign of doing so yet. ∆

Notes
1. Fredrick Kiesler, 'Notes on architecture as sculpture', *Art in America*, May 1966.
2. Fredrick Kiesler, 'Organic building – the city in space-functional architecture', *De Stijl*, 1925.

Below
Hastings This project is a new visitor centre combined with mixed-use facilities for the seafront in Hastings, England. Its form is inspired by the beautiful curves that a full net of fish creates as it is being hauled in. Its facade is created in weatherboarding to set up a resonance between itself, the hulls of boats and the cladding of net huts. The project attempts to create a gateway to the Hastings maritime area and its form, which some ungenerous critics have called scatological, cossets external terraces that open themselves up to the city and the coast. It is a bold and inventive approach that aims to reconcile not only the change in urban grain but also the materiality of the area with a project of this size and dynamism. If built, this might do to Hastings what Frank Gehry has done to Bilbao, but in a subdued, provincial, English way – not much trumpeting and a few scared councillors to boot.

Résumé Findlay

1979	Graduated from the Architectural Association in London	70
1980	Received a scholarship from the Japanese Ministry of Education for postgraduate research at the University of Tokyo	80
1980–82	Worked for Arata Isozaki and Associates	
1987	Findlay and Eisaku Ushida established the Ushida Findlay Partnership in Tokyo	
1989	Echo Chamber, Japan. Residential	
1993	Truss Wall House, Japan. Residential	90
1993	Chiaroscuro, Japan. Residential	
1994	Soft and Hairy House, Japan. Residential	
1995	Kaizankyo, Corporate, Japan. Retreat	
1998	Associate Professor of Architecture at Tokyo University until July 2001, where she supervised a design research laboratory (the first foreigner and first woman ever to hold such a position)	
1999	Visiting Professor of Architecture at UCLA	
2000	Kasahara Amenity Hall, Community Hall	00
2000	Bankside Loft, London. Interior fit-out	
2000	Homes for the Future, Glasgow	
2000	Hackney City Learning Centre, London. Educational Computer Space	
2000	Honorary Professor at the University of Dundee	
2001	Visiting Professor to the Technical University in Vienna	
2001	Grafton New Hall. Second-stage shortlisted, pending result	
2001	Claydon Heeley Jones Mason, London. Office fit-out	
2001	Poolhouse, Home Counties	
2001	House in Chelsea, London	
2002	Science/IT Lab at Graveney School.	

Below
Aerial view of the site looking northeast over the Yarra river. Federation
Square lies within the city-centre grid, which was laid out in the 1850s
when Melbourne became wealthy during Australia's gold rush.

Federation Square, Melbourne

Jeremy Melvin looks at the way
the new large-scale cultural
complex in Melbourne by Lab
architecture studio in association
with Bates Smart simultaneously
uncovers Australia's latent energy
whilst directly engaging with
the city's formal, public face.
A complex architecture of fractals
and 'differences', it playfully
responds to its setting in the
centre of Melbourne.

Below
Composite plan at level 2. Just as the facades have a common family of shapes, textures and materials, so the plan forms also show a resemblance, despite different conditions and functions.

Bottom
Composite plan of plaza level at ground level and one level above. The plaza assumes a form around the new institutions and existing energies of the city.

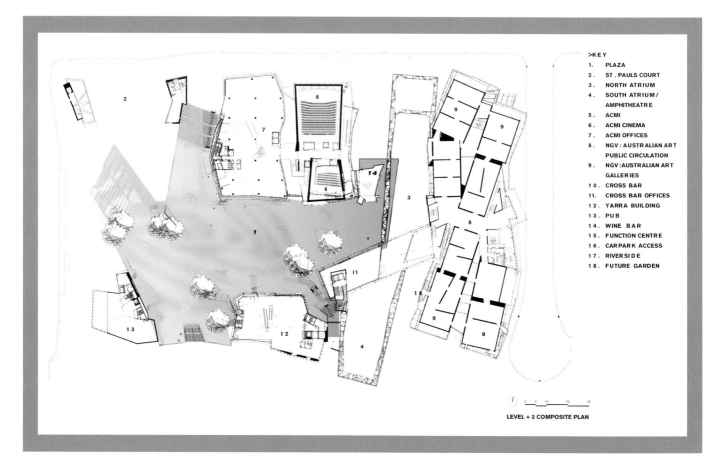

>KEY

1. PLAZA
2. ST. PAULS COURT
3. NORTH ATRIUM
4. SOUTH ATRIUM / AMPHITHEATRE
5. ACMI
6. ACMI CINEMA
7. ACMI OFFICES
8. NGV: AUSTRALIAN ART PUBLIC CIRCULATION
9. NGV: AUSTRALIAN ART GALLERIES
10. CROSS BAR
11. CROSS BAR OFFICES
12. YARRA BUILDING
13. PUB
14. WINE BAR
15. FUNCTION CENTRE
16. CARPARK ACCESS
17. RIVERSIDE
18. FUTURE GARDEN

LEVEL + 2 COMPOSITE PLAN

Australia is a country where architecture of any sort will always be incongruous, having to compete with spectacular scenery, a warm climate, sharp sunlight and a powerful myth-making apparatus that resides on the cricket square, beach or Australian-rules football pitch. Yet the approach Peter Davidson and his partner Don Bates at Lab architecture studio followed at Federation Square in Melbourne allows them to uncover this latent energy and to engage directly with the city's formal, public face. 'What interests us,' says Davidson, 'is how to find the really dynamic genetic coding of a city, not its formal and dead geometry'. So rather than follow the city centre's rigid grid they developed 'connectivity to the street system', the network of arcades and lanes that interweave with the imposed abstract geometry.

As their indented fractal facades play with sun and shadow, and the panels repeat in self-similar forms, the buildings across the complex, mainly cultural facilities with some commercial space, imply a dynamism and energy that could be a direct challenge to the formal orthodoxies represented by the grid. Despite its size, it is 'adjustable and manipulable at the level of small, minor connections to the city', says Davidson, alluding to 'inflections and views through'. The affinities go further: 'People think the colours [of the stone facades] pick up on the colours of the city', he continues. The structured informality extends to the shape of the plaza, a stepped public space that links the principal buildings and merges into

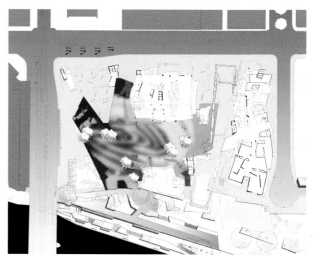

Below
View of the plaza looking east. By subtle inflections Federation Square seems to inhabit and encapsulate the city's form and character.

Bottom
Detail of artwork in the plaza showing texts by Peter Carter. These texts, part of an overall work called *nearamnew*, seek to represent the numerous cultural encounters in this location, a living embodiment of the project's functional programme.

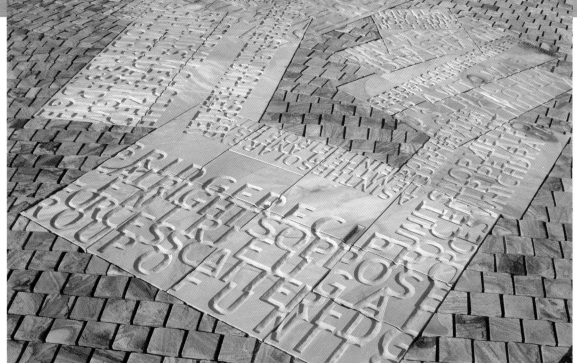

Below
ACMI southern facade facing the plaza. Using computer power to exploit complex
mathematical concepts in folding and surfaces, the facade systems celebrate the
possibility of combining coherence and difference.

Bottom
Section through atria. Above, looking west with south atrium and raked seating
to the left and north atrium interior to the right. Below, looking east. The
complex sits above the main commuter rail terminus.

Below
ACMI southern facade facing the plaza. Using computer power to exploit complex mathematical concepts in folding and surfaces, the facade systems celebrate the possibility of combining coherence and difference.

Bottom
Section through atria. Above, looking west with south atrium and raked seating to the left and north atrium interior to the right. Below, looking east. The complex sits above the main commuter rail terminus.

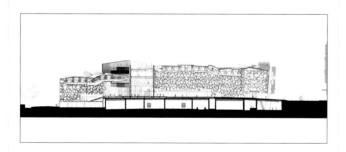

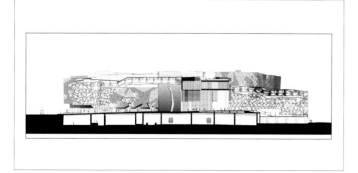

connections to the rest of the city. As the complex surfaces of the buildings make highly specific instances of their locations by their interaction with sunlight, so the surface of the plaza embeds a series of tablets the texts of which relate to the history of the site, bringing forgotten stories to public notice.

Federation Square, which Lab architecture studio won in competition in 1997, is part of a major renewal of Melbourne's sporting and cultural infrastructure over the last 10 years, and specifically marks the centenary of Australia's federation. This brought certain expectations: 'We were criticised for not having a statue of the founding fathers', explains Davidson, 'we would always say there were founding mothers as well'. More seriously, they see federation as 'projective not commemorative', rather as the progenitors of the United States saw their constitution as a blueprint for a country. The question was 'how to embody these principles in a way that would make them work'. Federation is about separate components that can develop independently. Davidson talks about simultaneous difference and coherence: themes and counterthemes can coexist. This, the pair argue, is far more appropriate to 21st-century Australia than representational art or traditional architecture that evokes the country's history.

Top
Exploded axonometric of the atrium structure.

Bottom
Node detail of the atrium structure.

Middle
Axonometric of the atrium structure. As in the fractal facades, each component is necessary
and its position contingent on the others, representing complexity but offering opportunity.

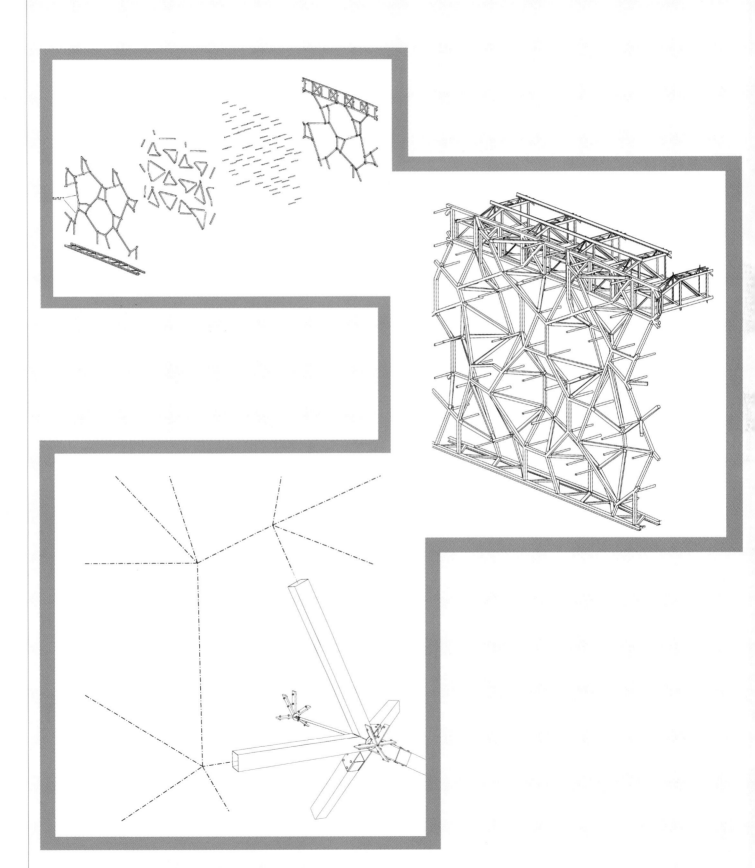

Top left
The NGV facade. Whether natural or artificial, light plays across the complex fractal facades, picking out their uniqueness and working with the signage to create a series of subtle ways of understanding the characters of the project's various components.

Top right
The facades are composed of identical triangular tiles, which are combined in fives to make a variety of panels. These panels can then be put together to make megapanels, giving almost infinite compositional possibilities within a standardised system.

Middle
South atrium at night. Within the softly illuminated environment, the atrium stands out. Even if it is not hosting an event it invites entry, mixing spontaneity with deliberation.

Bottom
The labyrinth walls take a zigzag form that doubles surface area and takes advantage of Melbourne's dry climate, which means temperatures drop at night and coolness can be stored to lower the air temperature within the atrium during the day, a solution devised in conjunction with Atelier 10.

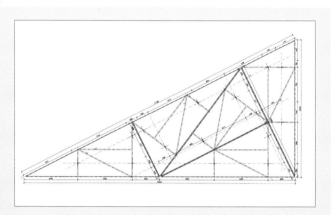

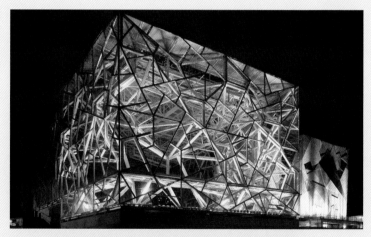

Some of these 'differences' were prefigured in the programme, which essentially sought to extend the public realm into the void above the main commuter railtracks with open space, new cultural institutions and some support from commercial and retail space alongside the Yarra river. The principal cultural institutions are the Australian Centre for the Moving Image (ACMI) and the National Gallery for the State of Victoria (NGV); within the plaza is an 'atrium', an extraordinary construction of fractal geometries and glass that manages to cool the outside air temperature. Other buildings include the 'shards' in front of Butterfield's St Paul's Cathedral, and the Yarra Building, which is designed for commercial lettings. This balance of uses immediately provides both difference and functional connections into the city; at least people go there for different reasons.

The design takes up this narrative. Each of the buildings and open spaces is irregular in form, making use of modern computing power that allows apparently complex forms to be simplified to a few repeated elements. This reaches its apogee in the facade system used on the ACMI, NGV and Yarra buildings. Triangular tiles can be combined in numerous ways to create a myriad of patterns across their facades. Using zinc, glass and sandstone means the textures vary too, and the surfaces undulate so that different parts reflect sky, sun and ground.

Yet all these 'differences' come from a rationalised production system and one single tile shape – five tiles make one panel, and panels make the facade – with an underlying coherence.

If the facade creates difference from similarity, the atrium takes the design further into the realm of the counterintuitive, a step which, like the reversal of the flow of the Chicago river or moving people underground, becomes entirely rational in a dense urban context. At its northern end a foyer to the NGV, and at the other an amphitheatre stepping down to the riverwalk, the atrium is a cool glass box, the structure of which is like a stack of tree trunks frozen immediately after the moment of explosion in a viscous solution.

In Melbourne, where temperatures can exceed 40°C, a glass box might overheat quickly, yet this is modulated to as much as 10°C below the outside temperature. Underneath is a labyrinth of concrete panels with serrated walls to increase surface area. At night cool air passes through the labyrinth so that it acts as a giant chiller during the day. This climatic effect makes the atrium a magnet during the day, and the way it reflects, refracts and transmits light turns it into a beacon at night against a softly illuminated background. These characteristics contribute to what Davidson describes as 'the subtle ways' in which people understand the forms, programmes and opportunities that Federation Square offers, and to the effect of being in an urban quarter where the threads of the city have been wound together and intensified.

This engagement with the city's inherent character is never literal but in one instance it becomes direct. Adjacent to Federation Square is the Anglican cathedral of St Paul's, designed by the great English Victorian Goth, William Butterfield. Butterfield did not want to replicate the relationship that Roman Catholic cathedrals have with their cities, standing at the head of a piazza. Instead he sited St Paul's off axis, within a block of the city grid, and it became embedded in the urban fabric. Federation Square gives it a new fabric, framing it between two 'shards' that contain the City Hub, an amalgam of Melbourne's visitor information services that brings something of the urban energy into the cathedral's precinct.

If this ties Federation Square into the city's formal and institutional life, its inhabitants ensure that it retains contact with Australia's informal and energetic lifestyle. Davidson marvels at the variety of activities in the plaza. By day it can hold many thousands who might congregate to watch the giant screen or for a planned event, yet by night it can be the scene of the most intimate moments. ⌂

Blurring the Lines:

An exploration of current CADCAM
techniques, parametric design and
rapid prototyping: mediating between
analogue and digital skill sets.

Parametric modelling is a powerful tool for analysis as well as invention of architectural form, as **Mark Burry** shows us in this second article of the 'Blurring the Lines' series through his work on the continuing construction of Gaudí's Sagrada Família Church. By embodying the architectural design as a system ('metaschema') of definable geometric relationships, we can reveal the cogency of even such an apparently expressionistically – some would say, 'arbitrarily' – sculpted edifice and improve the building by blurring the lines between the work of architect, engineer and mason.

As parametric design, a modus operandi sometimes more usefully referred to as associative geometry modelling, becomes more widely recognised as a potentially powerful ally for the architecture-engineering-construction (AEC) sector, we can begin to look for a more mature debate on its usefulness. It is interesting that a software paradigm that has been fairly well appreciated by the vehicle- and product-design industries for more than a decade has not stimulated more curiosity from building designers. High cost has been an obstacle certainly, but there may also be issues such as the risk of 'loss of authorship' impacting on its take-up, especially by architects more senior in years and not especially disposed to consider that the 'A' within the CAD acronym stands for 'aided', not 'automated'.

Just to recap the current state of play with parametric design, a software type that is fundamentally different from typical architectural CAD packages: its 'out of the box' state of development still provides little more than an arrangement for associating discrete geometrical elements inter alia within digital 3-D models. A cylinder of a certain length, for example, can have that length altered parametrically, that is to say by a variety of means either visually through interaction with the keyboard, monitor and mouse in combination, or by direct access to the database that contains information that can be updated externally while a model is being constructed. In either approach, rather than delete the cylinder and model a new one in order to alter a dimension – the only way to approach change in the majority of architectural packages – a dimension can be altered on the fly.

Some packages that include aspects of this facility have begun to emerge for architectural applications – parametric design at its most basic. Greater sophistication comes when discrete elements of geometry can be linked within the database, in other words attributes of one geometrically driven construct can be linked to another. In the case of the cylinder example above, the given length dimension could be set as being the same as the diameter of a sphere elsewhere in the model. If the length of the cylinder is increased, the diameter of the sphere increases accordingly.

The Sagrada Família Church in Barcelona has pioneered the AEC use of a high-end parametric design software intended for use by the aeronautical industry and manufacturing. The recently completed rose window has over 3800 separate such geometry linkages within the single parametric model for the whole highly complex window. This window was the first major element of the building to be based on Gaudí's general vision for the design for the church as a whole, but without the original large-scale modelled material from Gaudí's own hand that had been exclusively guiding the project under construction since his death – a resource that has now virtually come to an end.

The starting point for the rose window – the key feature for the passion facade (western transept) as it has an interior as well as an exterior presence – was a loose-fit, incomplete 1:25 gypsum plaster model made by Gaudí's successors in a number of interventions during the three-quarters of a century since his death. The challenge for the team based in Australia was to work from the loose-fit, incomplete compositional basis of the original model reaching out to an intellectually justifiable, iteratively sought definitive design that at once would marry Gaudí's use of second-order geometry to the overall design context.

Parametric design was a crucial aid in the case of this window for a number of reasons. Firstly, the 35-metre-high window had to emerge from the scaffolding fully glazed in a little over 12 months from the start of the work on the definitive design. Secondly, not only are the passion facade towers a little out of alignment, there is also an asymmetrical relationship between each set of two towers making the total group of four towers, and this asymmetry impacts on the otherwise symmetrical composition of the window. Therefore, to save time only one-half of the window was modelled: parametric design processes allowed a fast and flexible approach to experimenting with the design to be undertaken, and at a practical level it also allowed the second side to be a copy of its complement, parametrically altered to meet the idiosyncrasies specific to its location, as outlined above, for its corresponding opposite.

Parametric design also allowed the window to be developed on a 'lean construction' (aka 'just in time') basis: rather than design the window in detail in its entirety from the outset, a metadesign schema was

Sagrada Família Church, Antoni Gaudí, building commenced 1882–
Mark Burry (Consultant Architect) with Jordi Bonet (Coordinating Architect and
Director) and Jordi Faulí (Project Architect).

Below left
Loose-fit schema modelled by Gaudí's immediate successors in gypsum plaster
at a scale of 1:25 (interior view).

Below right
3-D parametrically based metadesign scheme for the (passion facade) rose window.

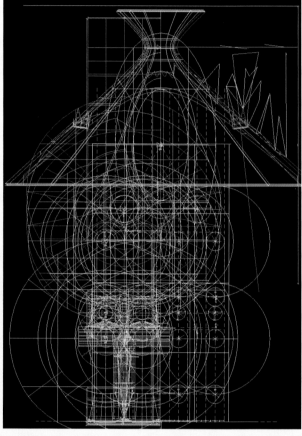

prepared for the window as a whole. Considering the window as approximately four horizontal divisions, the lowest quarter, having been detailed in Australia, was being constructed on site from individual granite elements made at the quarry in Galicia more than a thousand kilometres away. Meanwhile, the next level up was being cut in Galicia while the third quarter was being templated in Australia and, simultaneously, the design of the top quarter was still being negotiated with the Catalan university team working on the ceiling vaults with which the window intersects. The towers, which are finished in rough-cut stone, taper in height. Aligning any particular detail of the window with the rude masonry, so that it was neither truncated nor too distant from the surface, was made possible by reconfiguring the model parametrically once the data became available and was factored in; the data became available as the scaffolding rose in height.

On the Sagrada Família Church, as on all contemporary buildings with demanding representation issues, many different software packages were required for the process from concept through to detailed design. Parametric design software, in this

case CADDS5, was but the first step. In an intense, initial six-week design phase the team was based on site in Barcelona focusing on the 3-D modelling of the project as a parametric design with the master mason from the other side of the country, Señor Manuel Mallo, who has more than 50 years of experience in stone work and who was visiting on a weekly basis.

During this time, once the generic parametric model of the whole had been completed we were able to make a series of practical decisions about how to actually execute the project. In consultation with the mason, the whole wall was resolved into pieces of appropriate proportions according to the sizes of stone extractable from the quarry, the working environment in the yard, transportability and crane tare using a model exported from CADDS5 to Rhino as 3-D elements. Once the schema for the resolution of the lower part of the wall was completed, the 3-D Rhino model was converted into a series of 2-D A0 template drawings that owed much to the 18th-century tradition

Below left
Rose window: 3-D digital representation of interior.

Below right
Rose window: 3-D digital representation of exterior.

Below middle
The 3-D digital model is derived from a sequence of parametrically controlled Boolean subtractions.

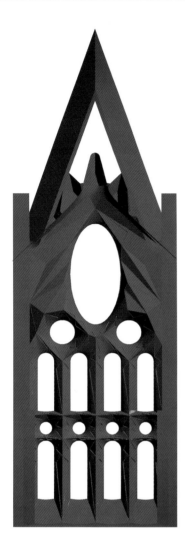

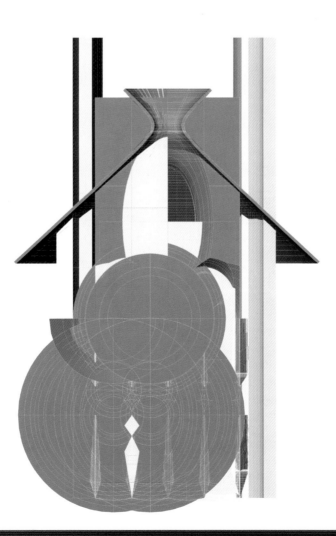

of traits – colours demarked actual stone faces, lines on the surface and coordinates. The more complicated pieces were prototyped from polystyrene at 1:1 scale. Contours at 10-centimetre intervals were included on the templates to describe the outlines of each layer of polystyrene prior to shaping. In this way, work could proceed around the globe so that the final design work of the upper level of the window could still be worked on parametrically while the lowest portion was being installed on site. This fast-track approach was possible only through the use of parametric design, and it allowed the stone mason to deploy his team of masons within three months of the design process commencing rather than wait for the whole design to be finished.

Parametric design has been impacting on the Sagrada Família Church in this way since 1992 when I was first introduced to the 'software style' by Robert Aish, the veteran campaigner for its development and take-up. His recommendation led to our implementation of a product apparently more suited to the aircraft industry than the building industry, and as a result Gaudí's unfinished magnum opus is the first example of an architectural 'total design approach' anywhere using such software. However, its use at the Sagrada

Família Church begs questions: can parametric design be used for the total design process or is it only usefully confined to resolving particularly complicated but nevertheless discrete building elements? Based on the evidence from our work for the Sagrada Família Church, we can at least demonstrate unequivocally its usefulness for the rapid design development, documentation and prototyping of discrete elements.

In the case of the rose window, proof of two improvements to the design-construct process emerged. The first is the opportunity for rapid design development. Each time we met on site, alternative design strategies could be tested parametrically in real time, thereby accelerating the normal change-represent-reflect-communicate cycle. We now communicate directly by Internet-based video conferencing, and in sharing our desktops across the globe we can effect parametric change in digitally shared work space and time. The second issue is the extraordinary increase in quality that results from specifically addressing conditions unknown at the time of design that normally result in what is often described

Below, anticlockwise from top left
Detail of geometry parameters, rendered outcome, typical AO
template, and example of a critical point parametrically varied to
meet the existing fabric perfectly once the data became available.

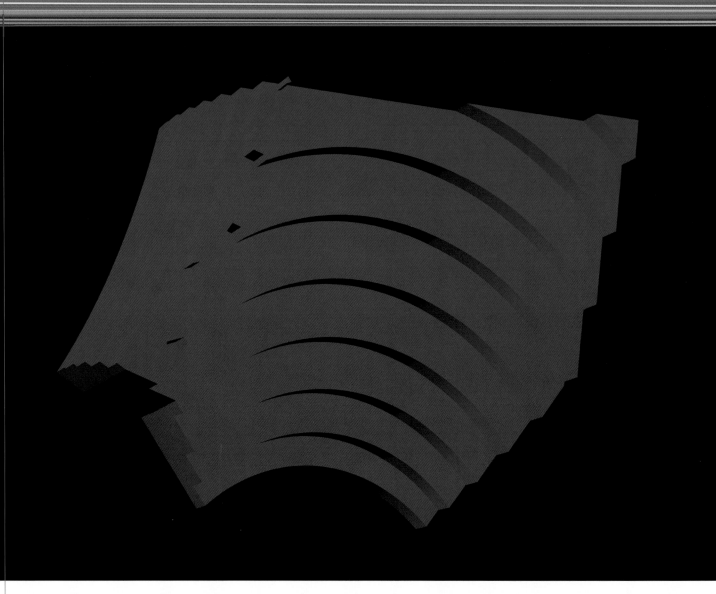

as 'fudging' outcomes. With a parametric model, as site circumstances become inevitably better understood during the construction process, adjustments can be made to the parametric model accordingly, giving greater accuracy and precision to the building information.

Beyond the Sagrada Família we are experimenting with parametric design in our research studio and in classes. Early indications suggest that it can significantly impact on total design practice and, interestingly, it can contribute to challenging 'sole-author hero' modes of operation, as seen with our collaboration with dECOi on a number of projects. Many unresolved issues still require significant research, most notably the metadesign issue, which is also described as 'designing the design'.

At the risk of contradicting the statement above, let me put this another way. If one individual makes a parametrically reconfigurable model in the way described above, it is unlikely that other individuals will be able to share the parametric potential of the model unless the author has taken the trouble to organise his or her design so as to be intelligible to his or her colleagues – some kind of strategic planning using

conventions understood by all the team. At once we can argue that parametric design aids collaboration and at the same time works against it. Part of our research has been to look at the development of meaningful protocols that encourage the sharing of the creative process rather than constrain it to the intellectual domain of one person. This metadesign issue also impacts on the model's ability to be reconfigured. And this introduces my final topic of constraint-driven design, where the constraints are designed in as creative elements and are not merely the result of protective individualistic authorship.

Let us return to the cylinder at the beginning of this piece. Constraints can be applied so that the length of the cylinder referred to earlier is set to be no more than 'x2' and no less than 'x1'. Deliberately hypothetically designed constraints can be linked too. We can set a condition that if the length of the cylinder, for instance, is more than a given value, the diameter of the sphere shifts from one relationship to another: this is managed

Below
Individual stone piece guided by mix of semi-automated and hand cutting via a 3-D
full-scale mock-up made from 2-D templates ('traits').

Bottom middle
Parametric design reconfiguration environment.

Bottom left
Parametric design 'history' showing relationships between decisions and outcomes.

Bottom right
10-millimetre gaps between adjacent stone pieces for tolerance proved
to be largely redundant given the inherent accuracy of the process.

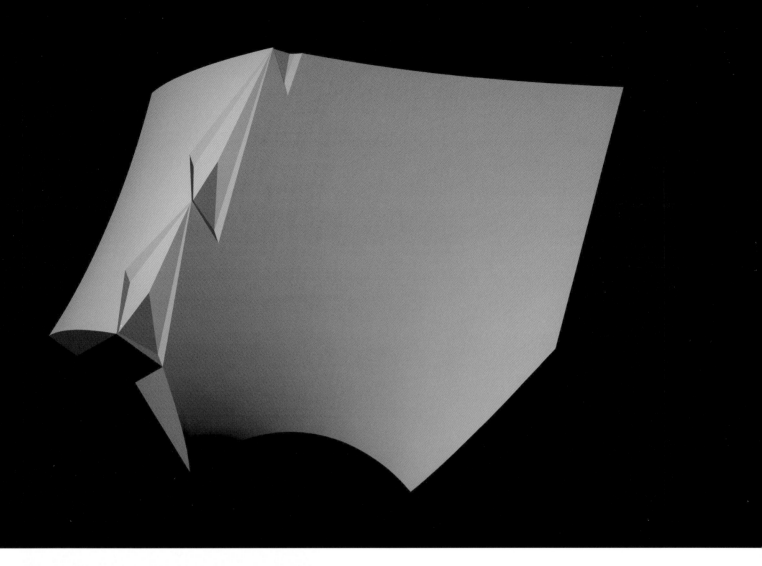

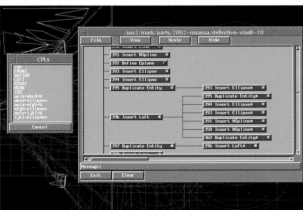

Below left and right
Two interior views of the glazed rose window partially occluded by
the platform supporting the construction of the ceiling vaults (2002).

by an equation or, with more sophistication, through the
application of logic programming. Although this is a trivial
example, mid- to high-level logic programming applied directly
to the parametric model yields fantastically powerful potential
for iterative design exploration and production. For this power
to be adequately realised, designers will need to rethink
their individual and collective approaches to setting out their
process, and architectural education be changed to suit. ∆

The research reported here has been part-funded by the
Australian Research Council. I also acknowledge the support
of the Junta Constructora of the Sagrada Família Church in
Barcelona for the opportunities they provide for us to do
extended research on the work of Gaudí in contemporary
architectural practice and research.

The application of parametric modelling to designing complex
metal fabrications will be the subject of Tim Eliassen's
upcoming article, in which we will also see the opportunities
and constraints inherent in working with materials that have
specialised technical demands.

The 'Blurring the Lines' series for Engineering Exegesis is edited
by André Chaszar, an engineer who combines independent
practice in New York with research into CADCAM techniques.

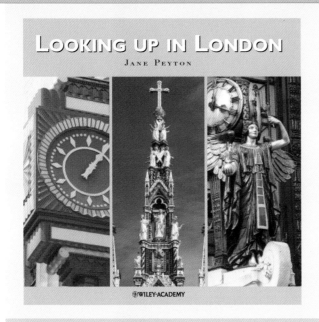

LOOKING UP IN LONDON
DISCOVERING A NEW WORLD IN A FAMILIAR PLACE
By Jane Peyton with photos by Helen Peyton

Your mission, if you choose to accept it, is to explore the architectural treasures featured in the book, *Looking up in London*. Imagine yourself as a detective and put your best sleuthing foot forward. You are on a journey to discover the incredible buildings that combine to make London such an unforgettable city.

This book is the key to a secret London. It will enable you to see the city as the people who scurry along streets looking straight ahead do not. Entering London's hidden world is simple, just look up above eye-level and prepare for a surprise. Giants, gargoyles, Greek gods and cherubs are gazing down, waiting to be admired.

Looking up in London was conceived twelve years ago when I walked along Moorgate and noticed several stunning building facades. From then on, my habits changed. If I was in an urban area, my eye-line never dropped below my shoulders, I took the bus rather than the Underground and when I was in the street with friends I started nudging them and saying "Oh look at that!" and rapturously gazing upwards. Virtually no-one else on the streets looked up at the hidden treasure. To me, London above eye-level deserved wider appreciation. The trouble with a book of photographs was that although they would be beautiful, such a collection might be limited to those with an interest in architecture. For a book to appeal to an audience that like me knew little about architecture but enjoyed looking at building facades it would need to contain more than just photographs. I designed the treasure hunt format so players would have fun whether they were architecture buffs or not as they discovered the building gems in the city.

I pitched the book without success, to countless publishers over a 12-year period. In that time I lived overseas and on each visit to London when I looked at all the marvelous hidden architectural gems it galvanized my determination to persevere until a publisher said yes.

It was a great feeling when Wiley - Academy commissioned *Looking up in London* and fantastic when my sister was chosen as the photographer. I moved back to England to start my research. From a long list of potential locations I had to reduce it significantly. Some of my favourite buildings were not included, either because they did not make good enough photographs or because they were in the wrong part of the city. Each building had to be geographically close, so readers could walk from one to another, always moving forward through London.

The book directs readers through eleven districts of central London. Along the route are the remarkable architectural treasures in the photographs. The goal is to find them, using the book as a guide. Accompanying each photograph are facts about the architect and architectural style. In addition, the book provides a brief historical portrait of each building.

To me, the City of London in particular is fascinating and researching the book has made it even more so. Visiting at the weekend when it is quiet, and walking through the maze of narrow streets brings the rich history of the City to life. No matter how many times I go, I always notice a building or detail that I have missed. If I had to choose one London street for fabulous facades, it would be Fleet Street. Almost every building is a gem.

Once you start looking up, you will be unable to stop, no matter where you are. *Jane Peyton*

Below
Jayne Merkel.

Bottom left and right
For the second issue of 2002, Jayne Merkel wrote a 'Practice Profile'
on New York office Caples Jefferson. The practice is joining Merkel
in the 2003 honours list in receiving an AIA Honors for Architecture.

Congratulations to
Jayne Merkel

In May 2003, Δ's Contributing Editor and Editorial Board Member
Jayne Merkel is to be awarded the prestigious AIA Institute Honors
for Collaborative Achievement by the American Institute of Architects
(AIA) at its annual conference in San Diego.

Below left
Jayne Merkel is currently combining her role on *Architectural Design*
with writing and researching a monograph on Eero Saarinen for
Phaidon Press. For the Furniture issue of △, she wrote a special piece
on the current revival of interest in Saarinen's furniture.

Below right
Issue of *Oculus*.

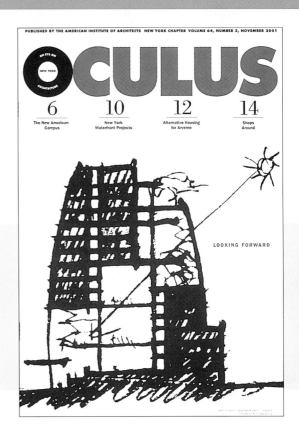

According to Bruce S Fowle, FAIA, in his nomination letter on behalf of the AIA Committee on Design:

> Jayne is the most prolific writer I know and is fully committed to comprehensive coverage of all the issues relating to the architectural industry. She is not just a superb architecture critic but also someone who comprehends and cares very deeply about the forces that shape our society.

The award goes some way towards recognising Merkel's substantial contribution to architecture as editor of *Oculus* (1994–2002). Until the demise of the print version in 2002, *Oculus* was a unique monthly magazine, published by the AIA New York Chapter. It covered all aspects of architecture in New York from the cultural through to the professional, as well as keeping astride of political and urban planning issues. Under her directorship, it became a focus for the architectural community in New York and an essential source for anyone else who wanted to know what was happening in architecture in the city. (Often *Oculus* was the original source for stories in *Time* and other international publications.) Paul Goldberger, architecture critic of the *New Yorker*, summarises Merkel's achievements as an editor:

> Jayne Merkel's *Oculus* has been a publication that you not only have to read but want to. She has managed the amazing trick of covering everything in New York without skimming too fast along the surface.

Cooper Union professor and architect Diane Lewis describes the important position Merkel cut out for *Oculus* during her eight years at the helm:

> *Oculus* gained a new presence in New York under her direction. As editor, Jayne further opened the debate on architecture in this city ... Alongside the *Times* and *New Yorker*, she proved that there is an important cultural position for *Oculus* – as a journal for the architects, by the architects.

Since producing the final print issue of *Oculus* in April 2002, Jayne Merkel has become a contributing editor to *Architectural Design*. She now writes for every issue. Her unique blend of journalistic skills, academic knowledge and natural curiosity give her a rare breadth. (She was the architecture critic of the *Cincinnati Enquirer* from 1977 to 1988 and director of the graduate program in Architecture and Design Criticism at the Parsons School of Design/New School University from 1992 to1996). She is able to write with some authority on subjects as diverse as fashion, restaurant design, digital architecture and social housing. She has already interviewed, among others for △: Steven Holl, Terence Riley, Diller + Scofidio, Bernard Tschumi and Yung Ho Chang.

Recipients will be presented with their awards in May 2003 at the AIA National Convention in San Diego, California. △ HC

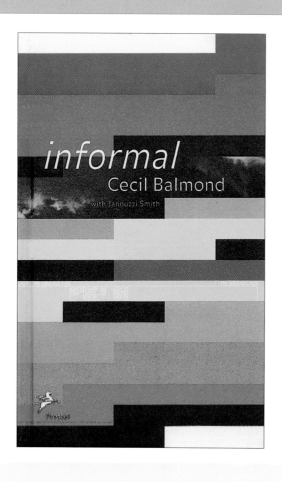

Invisibly Informal

On the publication of Cecil Balmond's new monograph *Informal*, Lucy Bullivant appraises Balmond's contribution to architecture and engineering.

To be told that 'your work is so invisible' by a fellow professional, and take it as a huge compliment, seems strange. Yet when it comes to Cecil Balmond – the London-based Sri Lankan structural engineer, Chairman of the European division of international firm of consulting engineers Ove Arup & Partners for the past 30 years and Saarinen Professor at Yale – the remark means that his original ideas about form have influenced his high-level collaborations with world-famous architects – without disturbing their egos. In fact, his collaborators queue to sing his praises. 'Perhaps as only a non-European could,' says leading Dutch architect Rem Koolhaas, 'Cecil has destabilised and even toppled a tradition of Cartesian stability'.[1]

These descriptions suggest a quietly subversive role for Balmond, a polymath who is passionate about the role of maths and music in the creative overlap between science and art. His organising skills in transforming line into plan and topology are much sought after and as far-sighted in design

terms, perhaps, as Kandinsky's point, line and plane art works were in the 1920s.

Providing the engineering wizardry behind some of the most advanced architecture in Western cities, Balmond's work includes James Stirling & Michael Wilford's 1984 Stuttgart Staatsgalerie, notably its complex collage of column/wall intersections; Rem Koolhaas's all-steel City Hall in the Hague (1988) and Kunsthal in Rotterdam, where structure is treated as episodes; 'a catalogue of juxtapositions', Congrexpo in Lille (1994); a trio of spaces with a hybrid rather than macro solution in a roof of timber and steel, the Jussieu Library in Paris, won in competition in 1996, with its spiralling floor ramps and permeable facade; and the Maison de Floriac in Bordeaux for a disabled owner, a new twist on the floating box.

For Daniel Libeskind's Imperial War Museum in Manchester (2001), Balmond helped to realise the

Below middle
Instead of structural framing like a 'regular monotonous beat of verticals and horizontals', Balmond advocates inclining the vertical, sloping the horizontal, or allowing 'two adjacent lines of columns to slip past us. Let space enlighten us'.

Below right
Sketches of the four proposals – brace, slip, frame and juxtaposition; structural ideas as a generating path to 'a hybridisation that wraps around the visitor'.

Opposite
Cover of *Informal*, Cecil Balmond's new monograph.

Below left
Rem Koolhaas, Kunsthal, Rotterdam, 1992, under construction.

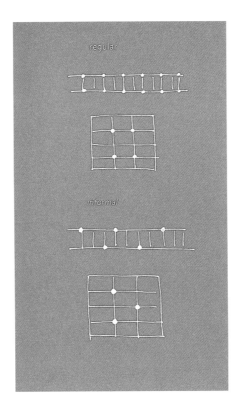

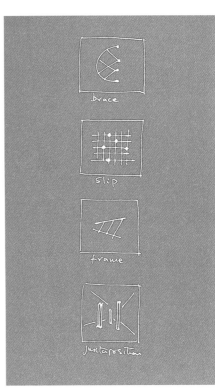

building's rationale of structured steel shells clad in concrete, supporting each other in interconnecting shards, and for the proposed Spiral building at the V & A there is the prospect of a 3-D wrap with self-stabilising walls with a fractal tile pattern. The bond between the architect and the engineer produces a consummation; however, it is hard for outsiders to truly gauge who did what. That is the art, as well as the risk, making Balmond's work a real balancing act. For Marsyas, the huge PVC membrane sculpture by the artist Anish Kapoor currently filling the turbine hall of the Tate Modern in London, Balmond makes the engineering invisible, building it into the structure that is the extraordinary art work that results and to which people respond immediately as they crane their necks: 'How did they do that?'.

Balmond is equally happy to work on small projects as his heavyweight urban interventions, such as the intimate cube pavilion jointly designed with Toyo Ito for the Serpentine Gallery in London last summer. Meanwhile, his list of forthcoming building commissions is sizeable. He is consulting engineer on Koolhaas's Seattle Library, its floating slabs of programme held together by a diagonal-meshed seismic system and, further into the future, a major scheme for a media headquarters in Beijing, UN Studio's Music School in Graz, Austria, which will feature a spiral that winds longitudinally, overlapping itself, and the transport interchange at Arnhem in the Netherlands, planned for completion in 2006 and

set to be the most ambitious demonstration yet of Ben van Berkel and Caroline Bos's adherence to seamless structures. And regarding Libeskind's new Denver Art Museum and Jewish Museum in San Francisco, each in their own way explores the interdependence of forms and the interplay of solids and their disappearance.

The structural engineer who Libeskind calls 'a thinker, a mystic'[2] has now written a book revealing the ideas behind his work. *Informal*, a small hardback with the weight and proportions of a brick (frankly, I was hoping for pop-up demonstrations and less weight, but maybe the light, physically emergent book will be Balmond's next one), is a sandwich of 'manifesto, theory and templates' and sensibly argues that architecture has to change in relation to society. Just as there is a wider breakdown in fixed ideologies, a more informal approach is called for in the built environment. For Balmond, 'informal' means natural patterns and energies must be co-opted into building to avoid standardisation and creeping soullessness. Koolhaas is thoroughly convinced: through Balmond's work, he claims in his preface to *Informal* that engineering can now enter a more experimental and emotional territory, one that helps architecture transcend its currently ornamental status.[3]

Below
Spiral building, V & A, London, ongoing, Daniel Libeskind, the spiral concept as generic, capable of many interpretations. Electing a generic initial configuration leads to the widest possible range of solutions.

Below
Portuguese Pavilion, Expo 1998, Lisbon, Alvaro Siza, a concrete canopy 20 cm thick and spanning 70 metres. At the last moment of span, just before the safety of the vertical anchors the catenary form is cut. Instead of a high tech answer or hangers, the curve itself is a structure in a heavy material to give balance against wind uplift, with ground beams acting as struts.

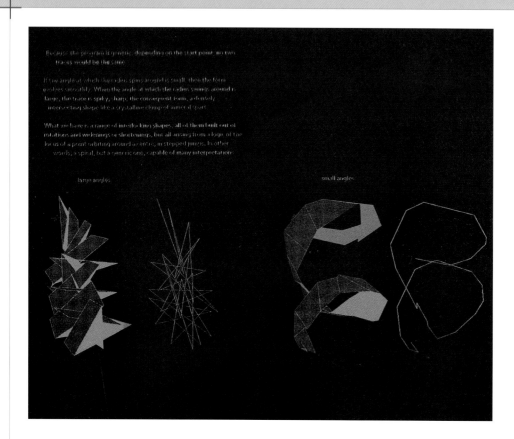

Taking Balmond's nonlinear approach, layering and folding form usurp the place of Newtonian mechanics, repetitive rhythm and hierarchy. It is an architectural vision of the complexity theory. 'The classical ideas of form we've all inherited, of symmetry, plan, boundary, I'm challenging that whole basis', he says. 'Why does space have to be container-like and neutered to house works of art?' Instead of the minimal modern, he opts for 'layered and more complex forms – not new, look at the brick patterning on Victorian facades – which give a deeper reading'. The design process, Balmond explains, embraces more – as desirable and different.[4] As Charles Jencks asserts in his introduction to *Informal*, the new is characterised by 'more is different',[5] a phrase of the Nobel laureate and scientist Philip Anderson, meaning that when you add more information or energy or mass to something, its system jumps into a new pattern of organisation. However, it must be digested to avoid pure collage. Don't be deceived: 'What is an improvisation is in fact a kernel of stability, which in turn sets sequences that reach equilibrium', says Balmond. Opportunistic, but not ad-hocist, his approach gives rise to ambiguity as one definition of an intense exploration of 'the intermediate', and simultaneity, in which several equilibriums coexist but never hierarchy.

Informal certainly employs a form of abstract mantra only a true cultural catalyst can get away with. It places the charting of the design process of 10 of Balmond's most creative collaborations with architects, shown step by step

in tiny sketches, in a metaphysical perspective the terms of which many architects would feel uneasy about arguing for, such is their level of pragmatism. Calling the creative dialogue between architecture and engineering 'the writing of new stories', he reveals how he makes shapes that defy gravity, are beautiful but also pragmatic and relate to their context. For instance, 'structure is flow' in Ben van Berkel's Arnhem interchange. The task being to integrate and make compatible three separate layers of programme, concourse area, basement car-park grid and commercial offices, Balmond and van Berkel avoided organising space in vertical slices and generated a mobility of plan with inclined V-walls. To keep the curvature as a 'natural consequence of the concept', the connecting roof and floors are merged into one network.

The tag of engineer as invisible creator does not appear to disturb Balmond; however he clearly enjoys writing about the design process: 'A lot of engineering assumes comprehensivity. It wants to be correct so it's hard to see a strategy that may have evolved, for instance with cascading load, where the structural systems are carried by each other, and are interdependent, or nonhierarchical, like Sydney Opera House'. The shared nature of the creativity behind such a creation is hardly part of the media narrative about

Below
Arnhem Interchange, Arnhem, completion 2006, UN Studio. A seamless structure, with one skin of concrete providing inclined walls, ramps and vaulting roof, and mixing separate 'strands' of cars, trams, buses and people. With such connectivity, zones of confluence, aggregations, overlaps and bandwidths become a new language for structure.

Composition is an overlayering of the seen versus the unseen with potentiality set against the real. What is left in the mind is something different to the canopy, a sculpture of another sort, an unfolding series of informal cuts in an imagined space.

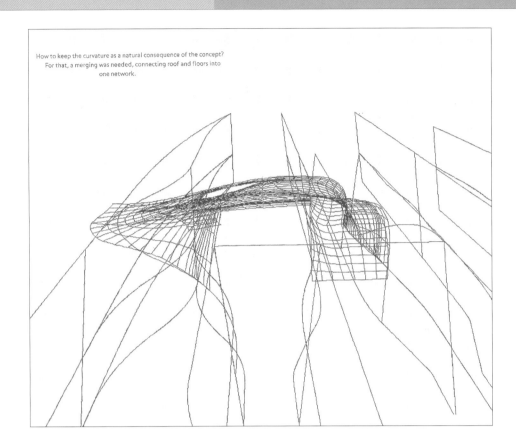

How to keep the curvature as a natural consequence of the concept? For that, a merging was needed, connecting roof and floors into one network.

the architectural star system; that's why it is worth paying attention to Balmond's comments.

Balmond argues that we are now in a period in which, as in the early Renaissance or the early 20th century, professional barriers are breaking down as specialists exchange roles. A revolution in built form is slowly developing that will hugely affect the appearance of cities in the future: 'We have not changed in 2000 years how we see form – as column and beam – but it is changing now. We are poised to go into a new paradigm of geometry'. So what effects does the breaking down of Cartesian form usher in? 'A sense of movement, a certain sensation, which you have in Koolhaas's villa in Bordeaux where the structure breaks with symmetry, and instead you have concepts of "slip, jump and overlap"'. This is not hi-tech architecture or purely sculpture masquerading as building, but about bringing a lyrical, metaphysical quality to the organisation of form and space. In this sense Balmond is in the tradition of the brilliant Italian bridge-builder Nervi rather than following the iconic, early modern aesthetic of Eiffel. Clients have said to him: 'I can't understand what's going on, but I know what it is, and it's joyful'.

A canopy in concrete at the Lisbon Expo '98 site for architect Alvaro Siza, for instance, has an equilibrium so simple it is like a Zen temple, one that hovers above the ground like a spacecraft: 'People don't know there's 2,000 tonnes of concrete, but it's only 20 centimetres thick'. With its taut curve, it splices substance with air, its structure 'a metaphysic in the science of architecture', flying like a bird.

Admittedly a dutiful 'problem solver' in his early career after graduating from Imperial College, Balmond soon began 'posing questions that were unanswerable'. His mind is, as his collaborators rely upon, 'wired to be subversive' and functions as an inventor. 'People are excited by the organisation of form in, say, the great cathedrals, as there's a mystery seeded to it. Each time you visit the dense field of columns of Cordoba's mosque, for instance, you see different things'. The intrigue of his work lies in the interdependence of the rational and the totally systematic with the mystical: 'I don't want people to think I do abnormal buildings. I can't remain poetic on the drawing, all the laws of physics have to apply'. His emerging 'informal' repertoire encourages even the sceptic that there is power in such intermediacy, and art and science are not really in conflict, but more meaningfully in love with each other. ⊅

Notes
1. Rem Koolhaas, 'Preface', in Cecil Balmond, Informal, Prestel Verlag (Munich, Berlin, London, New York), 2002, p 9.
2. Quoted in Jennifer Kabat, 'The Informalist', Wired, June 2001.
3. Koolhaas, op cit.
4. Cecil Balmond, Berlin, 1995, quoted in Informal, pp 219–27.
5. Charles Jencks, 'Changing Architecture', introduction to Informal, p 7.

Lucy Bullivant is the guest-editor of Home Front: New Developments in Housing, the July/August 2003 issue of Architectural Design.
Cecil Balmond, Informal, Prefaces by Charles Jencks and Rem Koolhaas, Prestel, £29.95, 400 pp.

Building Exploratory

Below left and right
Model of Cedar Court, Holystreet Estate in the London borough of Hackney
Designed by artist/sculptor James MacKinnon in association with Tom
Hunter (interior photography) and Mike Seaborne (exterior photography).

Hannah Ford, the author of a new book on architecture centres, describes the Building Exploratory in Hackney, London.

Public interest in architecture has risen in recent years; combined with social developments of increased democracy, citizenship and public participation, a need for independent organisations to facilitate this has arisen. Architecture centres have been established for a wide range of reasons; many are local centres, which engage with local planning and architectural issues and with the general public including children. Their independent status gives them a political edge and a critical voice.

In the London Borough of Hackney, the Building Exploratory is an architecture centre whose contents engage the public through hands-on resources, a highly illuminating experience, which is educational at heart. An architecture centre of this kind enables people to begin to see why it is they themselves that bring the public realm alive. The taking part on this level is one entry into the democratic process and a way to begin to understand the wider issues that will affect local communities. And in turn, the group of stakeholders begin to be more inclusive; it is people that shape the built environment. And it is this simple fact that is often forgotten when buildings are being built.

As is the case with many architecture centres around the country, the Building Exploratory receives little regional or national government funding and is therefore dependent upon sponsorship, grants, goodwill and local support. Due to the unstable nature of funding many architecture centres in England rent spaces in existing structures. There are a few exceptions; The

Below left
3D model of the London borough of Hackney developed and
built by schoolchildren. 360 children from eight local schools
in Hackney have gradually built the model over time.

Below right
Journey to the centre of the Earth starting
from the London borough of Hackney.

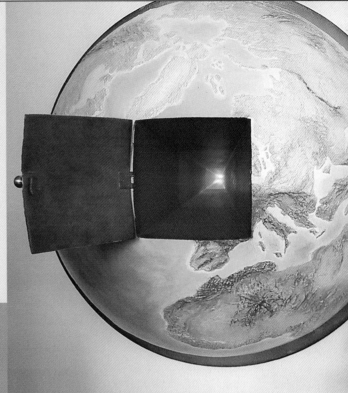

Lighthouse in Glasgow, the Bristol Architecture Centre and
CUBE (Centre for the Urban and Built Environment) in
Manchester all received Lottery funding to renovate former
buildings to fit their new function. The Exploratory, however,
occupies one floor of an archetypal Victorian school building.
It also operates as an adult education centre and a nursery
school. Established in 1997, the Exploratory chose Hackney
because of its fascinating local history and as one of 33 London
boroughs it also has the highest percentage of social housing
in all boroughs – 70%. The Exploratory was conceived
and designed to help local communities understand and
appreciate their area, and to feel empowered by the process
of engagement in the urban environment. One day, it is
envisioned that each borough will have its own Building
Exploratory.

Each visitor to the Exploratory will see themselves
somewhere in the exhibits, they will see how and at what level
they can and do make an intervention into the public realm.
The most moving exhibit is a model of a tower block, an exact
replica of the former Cedar Court building on Holystreet
Estate built by Hackney Council in the 1960s. In 2001, the
block was condemned and seen unfit to live in. It was riddled
with 'concrete cancer', first diagnosed at Pruitt Igoe, tower
blocks in St Louis, which were demolished in 1972 marking
the beginning of the end of Modernism's contribution to social
engineering.

After re-housing its former tenants, Hackney Council blew
up the block, along with a second out of three shortly after.
However, before the final curtain, the Exploratory
commissioned the artist James MacKinnon to make a replica

model of Cedar Court complete with interior decoration,
wallpaper, lights, lifts, rubbish chutes, windows and
concrete. The model allows you to be highly voyeuristic,
peering into the tiny flats on every floor – some with
flock wallpaper, others completely sparse, and,
shockingly, one flat completely burnt out. Holystreet
Estate is survived by one tower block, recently
refurbished with living rooms extended out to the
balconies and facilities back in full working order.
By simple maintenance, its revival has been considered
a success by the local community. The model serves
as a record of the built environment in Hackney and why
the landscape changes. It allows community members
– schoolchildren to pensioners – to visit the Exploratory
in order to view and begin to understand the topology
of building types from different centuries on display.
But most importantly, it is to represent and value their
contribution to public space equal to an architect or
urban planner visiting the centre.

Public participation, education, collaboration and
debate are common themes for all architecture centres
in this country and abroad. But while the Building
Exploratory operates an exhibition programme, public
participation doesn't stop there. Architecture centres
encourage people to engage actively in public realms
that test new ideas, criticise or celebrate, and allow
new thinking about the environment to take place. ᴐ

To read more about architecture centres from around the world,
see *International Architecture Centres* edited by Hannah Ford and
Bridget Sawyers, published by Wiley-Academy.

Subscribe Now for 2003

As an influential and prestigious architectural publication, *Architectural Design* has an almost unrivalled reputation worldwide. Published bimonthly, it successfully combines the currency and topicality of a newsstand journal with the editorial rigour and design qualities of a book. Consistently at the forefront of cultural thought and design since the 1960s, it has time and again proved provocative and inspirational – inspiring theoretical, creative and technological advances. Prominent in the 1980s for the part it played in Postmodernism and then in Deconstruction, ⟁ has recently taken a pioneering role in the technological revolution of the 1990s. With groundbreaking titles dealing with cyberspace and hypersurface architecture, it has pursued the conceptual and critical implications of high-end computer software and virtual realities. ⟁

⟁ Architectural Design

SUBSCRIPTION RATES 2003
Institutional Rate: UK £160
Personal Rate: UK £99
Discount Student* Rate: UK £70
OUTSIDE UK
Institutional Rate: US $240
Personal Rate: US $150
Student* Rate: US $105

*Proof of studentship will be required when placing an order. Prices reflect rates for a 2002 subscription and are subject to change without notice.

TO SUBSCRIBE
Phone your credit card order:
+44 (0)1243 843 828

Fax your credit card order to:
+44 (0)1243 770 432

Email your credit card order to:
cs-journals@wiley.co.uk

Post your credit card or cheque order to:
John Wiley & Sons Ltd.
Journals Administration Department
1 Oldlands Way
Bognor Regis
West Sussex PO22 9SA
UK

Please include your postal delivery address with your order.

All ⟁ volumes are available individually. To place an order please write to:
John Wiley & Sons Ltd
Customer Services
1 Oldlands Way
Bognor Regis
West Sussex PO22 9SA

Please quote the ISBN number of the issue(s) you are ordering.

⟁ is available to purchase on both a subscription basis and as individual volumes

○ I wish to subscribe to ⟁ *Architectural Design* at the **Institutional rate of £160.**

○ I wish to subscribe to ⟁ *Architectural Design* at the **Personal rate of £99.**

○ I wish to subscribe to ⟁ *Architectural Design* at the **Student rate of £70.**

STARTING FROM ISSUE 1/2003.

○ Payment enclosed by Cheque/Money order/Drafts.

Value/Currency £/US$ [   ]

○ Please charge £/US$ [   ] to my credit card.
Account number:

[ ][ ][ ][ ][ ][ ][ ][ ][ ][ ][ ][ ][ ][ ][ ][ ]

Expiry date:

[ ][ ][ ][ ][ ]

Card: Visa/Amex/Mastercard/Eurocard *(delete as applicable)*

Cardholder's signature [   ]

Cardholder's name [   ]

Address [   ]

[   ]

[Post/Zip Code   ]

Recipient's name [   ]

Address [   ]

[   ]

[Post/Zip Code   ]

I would like to buy the following Back Issues at £22.50 each:

○ ⟁ 161 *Off the Radar*, Brian Carter + Annette LeCuyer

○ ⟁ 160 *Food + Architecture*, Karen A Franck

○ ⟁ 159 *Versioning in Architecture*, SHoP

○ ⟁ 158 *Furniture + Architecture*, Edwin Heathcote

○ ⟁ 157 *Reflexive Architecture*, Neil Spiller

○ ⟁ 156 *Poetics in Architecture*, Leon van Schaik

○ ⟁ 155 *Contemporary Techniques in Architecture*, Ali Rahim

○ ⟁ 154 *Fame and Architecture*, J. Chance and T. Schmiedeknecht

○ ⟁ 153 *Looking Back in Envy*, Jan Kaplicky

○ ⟁ 152 *Green Architecture*, Brian Edwards

○ ⟁ 151 *New Babylonians*, Iain Borden + Sandy McCreery

○ ⟁ 150 *Architecture + Animation*, Bob Fear

○ ⟁ 149 *Young Blood*, Neil Spiller

○ ⟁ 148 *Fashion and Architecture*, Martin Pawley

○ ⟁ 147 *The Tragic in Architecture*, Richard Patterson

○ ⟁ 146 *The Transformable House*, Jonathan Bell and Sally Godwin

○ ⟁ 145 *Contemporary Processes in Architecture*, Ali Rahim

○ ⟁ 144 *Space Architecture*, Dr Rachel Armstrong

○ ⟁ 143 *Architecture and Film II*, Bob Fear

○ ⟁ 142 *Millennium Architecture*, Maggie Toy and Charles Jencks

○ ⟁ 141 *Hypersurface Architecture II*, Stephen Perrella

○ ⟁ 140 *Architecture of the Borderlands*, Teddy Cruz

○ ⟁ 139 *Minimal Architecture II*, Maggie Toy

○ ⟁ 138 *Sci-Fi Architecture*, Maggie Toy